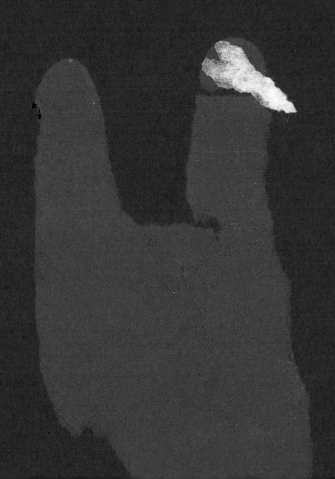

COYOTE

Coyote

SEEKING THE HUNTER
IN OUR MIDST

CATHERINE REID

Houghton Mifflin Company

BOSTON   NEW YORK   2004

Visit our Web site: www.houghtonmifflinbooks.com.

Library of Congress Cataloging-in-Publication Data

Reid, Catherine, date.
Coyote : seeking the hunter in our midst / Catherine Reid.
p.   cm.
ISBN 0-618-32964-1
1. Coyote.   I. Title.

QL737.C22R438   2004
599.77'25 — dc21   2004047494

Book design by Anne Chalmers
Drawings by Jared T. Williams
Typeface: Janson Text

Printed in the United States of America

QUM 10 9 8 7 6 5 4 3 2 1

To my parents,
Bob and Marjorie Reid,
for their expansive,
generous love

The coyote . . . is
a living, breathing
allegory of Want.

— Mark Twain,
Roughing It

COYOTE

I

AFTER TWO MONTHS in this old house, I think I know the night noises at last — the knock and scramble of mice in the walls, the huff of wind across the chimney, the bristle of windows within their loose frames. Yet tonight comes a cry that I wasn't expecting, that hauls me out of sleep, a chorus of wailing above a percussion of yips, excited and eerie and twitching my heart.

Coyotes. Their very existence makes this place seem risky and wild. I hadn't reckoned on their presence when we made an offer on the place. Carpenter ants and powder-post beetles, flying squirrels and foraging deer, gray squirrels fattened on acorns and birdseed, plenty of roaming bear — these were the known parts of the package, along with what we could see for rot in the sills, what we hoped was solid framing behind the new siding, and what we couldn't quite follow in the network of old knob-and-tube wiring.

But at the thought of a pack of coyotes — a gang, a family — another sensation crawls across my skin, like knowing someone is behind a door before a hand can slam it shut.

I want to see them.

I want to find their outlines when I scan the edges of the meadow. I want to know if I'm being watched while I work in the garden or mow the field. I want to know where they sleep and spend their days, where they go when the neighboring dogs race through or when November arrives after the leaves have blown free and hunters slip into the newly naked woods.

Mostly I want to know how they're managing here in Massachusetts, in this place I've returned to twenty-five years after leaving. Coyotes were just sliding into the landscape back then, rarely seen and seldom heard, and only starting to appear in northern Vermont, where I first lived as a young adult. I saw them sometimes from a distance. I heard them now and again at night, that same rupture of my sleep, something separate from the weave of other sounds. And once I met a coyote in a field, each of us too distracted by the hot August buzzing to notice the other until we were both in full view. Without taking its eyes from me, it did a slow turn, lowered itself into the grass, and disappeared. I backed up to the field's edge, to the shadow of a big rock maple, and waited for an hour. It didn't return; its shape never reformed inside that dense weave of grass.

I want to know how they disappear like that.

THOSE OF US who decide to return home run certain risks. We lose the luster of the one who got away, the status that accrued when no one really knew what we did with our time. We no longer feel free to move on whenever plans change, a relationship doesn't work out, another job beckons from somewhere farther afield. We become accessible and known and have to face tomorrow the mistakes we make today.

For me, being home again means having to bridge the gaps between the kid I was when I left and the adult I've become. That seems most obvious when my tender-hearted father calls and leaves a message on the machine. "It's your daddy," he says, his voice as it was when I was five and six and seven, not that of a man in his seventies addressing his fortysomething daughter. Later, when our paths cross in town, the joy on his face feels equal to my own at the unexpected chance to catch up on more of what we missed during all those years we spent so far apart.

It's the same with my five siblings when we jostle and tease each other as we did when we were teens; then we step back and wonder when the gray crept in and the wrinkles inched across our faces. All of them have kids now, ranging in age from one to eighteen, children amiable and curious, though I can't tell yet if any have a name for the aunt who came back with her companion, a woman with a past that is full and unknown to them. It's partly Yankee reticence, this reluctance to talk about the less visible part of our lives; it's partly a wish not to be misunderstood. But it might also indicate how much has changed since that day I left in order to become my whole self.

"You'll never be able to move back home," a former partner once told me, and I believed her. She was older, and I thought she was wiser; she studied family relationships as part of her job. Years passed before I understood that by saying I'd be smothered by the traditions that abound here, she meant she was afraid of what they might do to her.

For me, fear that I couldn't be myself was a natural consequence of years bounded by tradition, centuries of Puritan-tight belts and stiff upper lips defining our options like lines of barbed wire inscribing old woods. As a teenager, however, I was oblivious to history's impact. Everything was new and possible, and I'd felt free to come and go as I wanted, to slip back and forth between adulthood and adolescence. Yet I was caught unawares by the arrival of a love I knew to be unlike any other I had experienced. I was even more startled by the reactions from those who had always encouraged me. They had never said *No*, they had never said *Don't*, so when they pulled back in anguish — *You can't love her!* — I was unmoored. The rope connecting me with the familiar had been cut, and a part of me folded up, a part that has often felt stranded in despair.

THE PROPERTY WE FOUND is in the hills of Franklin County, with the summits of the Berkshires a few miles to the west and the taller mountains of Vermont just to the north. To the east a short downward slope separates us from the flat expanse of the Connecticut River valley. As a child growing up near the river, I was sure that the hill people had far sturdier and more inventive lives than those of us stuck on flatter land. But after high school I never spent much time here, except for the year I hiked north with spring, from Georgia to Maine along the Appalachian Trail. By the time I reached New England, I had been out for about three months and loved being back within reach of familiar-sounding towns — Stockbridge, Dalton, Pittsfield, North Adams — enjoying the resonance of known accents and idioms, the way words like "the Berkshires" felt in my mouth. But I never thought I would live here, that the pull of home would be so strong, hauling me back from a thousand miles away.

A selling point of the property was that it had not one but three structures: an old farmhouse, a barn, and a much smaller building, about seventy-five feet across the lawn. We designated it the studio, and I won the coin toss for its use. A previous owner had run a small-engine repair shop out of it; another had sold used books. The latter must have been the one who had it wired and insulated, had a phone line brought in, had the walls covered with Sheetrock and painted. No one ever dealt with the concrete floor, however, which sloped toward a drain at its center.

Another benefit of moving back was that my siblings had most of the necessary skills for building or repairing whatever we wanted to fix. My youngest brother, Doug, spent much of his vacation time showing me how to erect jacks in the cellar under overly long joists and how to refinish the banged-up wood floors. We also spent hours in the studio leveling sleepers across the concrete floor and securing them with a gunpowder-driven hammer, each slam like a pistol going off in the small building. We fitted tongue-and-groove birch plywood on top, and immediately the room felt warmer and tighter. When his vacation ended and we were on our own, I continued to borrow Doug's tools and seek advice over the phone.

My brother Arthur helped as well, mostly by explaining how things worked. He reassured me about the knob-and-tube wiring, the gas heater in the studio, the buckling wall at the bottom of the barn. "And that's probably an old well cover," he said of the large, flat fieldstone in the barn floor. He offered to help lift it when I was finally curious enough. Then my oldest brother, Bob, brought two of his sons and a high-sided truck to the place we rented while readying the property, and their energy and hustle (sparked by the promise of a swim in the river) made the move to Shelburne Falls seem easy.

I like knowing that they are all close and would help in any way they could. But I need to sort out the rest of this on my own; it's how I learn. It's how I figure out what it will take to support my life. With the paint dry and the boxes emptied, I don't need to be inside the house any longer. It's time to learn the lay of this land.

I wander through the field to the narrow trail I found when first walking the property lines, which are defined mostly by old stone walls and a seasonal, moss-lined trickle. Two neighboring dogs use the path most often, but one morning last week I saw a young buck on it about to step into the field. We stopped at the same time to watch each other, but I relented first and slipped into the studio. From a shadow by the window I kept track of the deer's indecision — forward, back, forward, back — until a door slammed behind me and it disappeared in a flash of white tail.

Today I follow the path over a hill of white pine. To the north is a gentle slope of mountain laurel and princess pine, partridge berry and rattlesnake plantain; a steady brook churns in the small valley below. The railroad tracks run along the woods to the east; beyond them lies the Deerfield River, the Massamet Ridge rising steeply just beyond it.

Most of this I recognize and take comfort in, despite the years I've been away. I like to think that my return here is fresh enough that familiarity won't lead me to have blind spots, that my powers of observation won't relax among smells and rhythms that soothe like nursery rhymes. Keeping watch for something as elusive as a coyote should keep me alert to nuance and able to locate signs different from the ones I once expected.

It's tricky — *I know this; do I know this?* — like trying to walk toe-heel down the trail, something I practiced for weeks as a kid when I wanted to walk as silently as the Indians I had read about. I can do it now if I concentrate, but my heel hits first when I look anywhere but at the trail ahead of me, which I keep doing until I'm almost home. It's when the house and the barn are within sight that I find the first sign in my search — coyote scat in the clearing under a large white pine.

It's easy to distinguish from that of a dog, which looks like reprocessed Alpo, or that of a fox, which is narrower and has less heft. This mass is stringy and long and full of apple seeds and cherry pits, tiny bones and maple seeds, and a piece of waxed paper, wrinkled and wedged between clumps of matted hair.

THE HOUSE Holly and I occupy was built in 1894, the year the last passenger pigeon was shot in Massachusetts and about fifty years after the state's last wolf was killed. I don't know when the barn that used to stand on this foundation was built, but in the years between the gray wolf's death and the raising of this house, a series of animals was driven out of the state: the last wild turkey, shot in 1851 and only recently reintroduced; the last mountain lion, killed in 1858; the last lynx, in 1860; the last marten, in 1880.

I think about little of this history when I check mouse traps in the cellar. Holes riddle the foundation, small, dingy tunnels that stretch out of sight, some of them large enough to accommodate weasels. It seems terribly fragile, stone on stone, a little mortar or whitewash in between, and above it a two-story house delicately placed on notched and pitted sills.

Two of the traps contain bodies, and I walk outside to toss

them into the thicket behind the barn. Then, curious, I force a path through the brush to see where the carcasses landed. Stiff blackberry thorns catch at my sweater, and I have to stop several times to unpin them. But when I reach the tall elderberry, I don't find any of the mice I've flung these last two months — two or three dozen total. Instead, I find one bedraggled, inedible mole and the telltale scat of coyotes.

They've been scarfing up small mouse bodies at night.

They've been within twenty-five feet of the house, maybe even closer, and I haven't seen or heard them. I've simply been the unwitting purveyor, rewarding their approach.

I feel the same mix of awe and caution that I did when I fed a fox from my hand during one of the springs I lived on Deer Isle, off the coast of Maine. A mother fox, her fur matted, her teats swollen, had barked me out of the house in her hunger. Curious as to what she would do, I set half my sandwich on a rock and walked away. She took it and ran. For the next several weeks I tossed her more chunks of sandwich or muffin whenever she appeared in the clearing. Then I bought her Milk-Bones, which she liked, and both of us began taking more time with the exchange (I didn't let myself think for long about the cost to her of such an association, about whether the next person she approached would hold food or a gun; I simply used her ragged belly as an excuse for the transactions). At last, instead of dropping the food in front of her, I kept it in my hand, and she scarcely hesitated before lifting it from my palm with her teeth.

My body didn't know whether to scream or laugh when she darted away. I could see only how she took it — sharp, white fox teeth, a breath away from my skin.

2

THIRTY YEARS AGO, people were already starting to comment that something odd was going on. Some new creature was in the hills, and it seemed bigger than a coyote and yet wasn't quite large enough to be a wolf.

I was in high school at the time. I welcomed uncertainty. I despaired that so little seemed changed after the assassinations and riots and burnings, after Vietnam tested all the relationships I cared about. In their wake, our options seemed more limited, what we could say and do unduly weighted. I craved some sort of shock to our sense of natural order, a phenomenon that couldn't be caught or mapped or explained. Had I been more specific, I might have said, *And let it be unruly and in our very backyards.* The subsequent rumor seemed too good to be true — a new canid had arrived, never before known in these parts. I thrilled at the idea of a creature rising out of the very landscape we had sought to control with bulldozers and fences and streetlights and dams, something that could startle us with its teeth and resilience and a howl that punctured sleep and sped up breathing.

Though I couldn't have fully articulated the idea at the time, I liked knowing that these animals flourished on the margins, the same edges I would soon be exploring — the outskirts and far reaches to which the gender outlaws gravitated (Provincetown, Key West, San Francisco, the far end of the park, the last beach beyond the dunes), where it was possible to see who was coming and what they might want when they arrived.

The coyotes sliding into the Northeast had traveled the softwood forests first, where there were plenty of hiding places under the thickly needled branches of spruce and balsam fir, and where they perfected the art of camouflage. Over the years they became bolder, shifting from dark to light, wet to dry, changing with the forests while continuing to find refuge along the multiplying margins. Soon they were skinnying through the ragged cover next to schools and cemeteries, alongside marshes and tidal flats, in the tangle of underbrush behind fire stations and mall parking lots. Each time a logging company, developer, road crew, or farmer changed the way the land was used, the coyotes accommodated, using the disruption to settle into the comfortable niche left vacant when the last wolves were driven from the region.

It's a different story, this slipping in, from the all-out rout of the wolves, which was fueled by the early settlers' hatred of them. From this remove, it's painful to hear the contrast between the stories of the Native Americans, in which the wolf figured as a powerful fellow creature, and those of the early Europeans, who saw it as a frightening competitor, a granny-eater and tempter of little girls, or as the sort of fiend that could eat every member of the wedding party when their sleighs overturned in deep snow. In other tales brought to the New World, wolves were known to transform into werewolves who danced and fornicated with the Devil; other wolves took the shape of men until marriage, when one might disappear into the night only to return years later, lice-ridden, hairy, and ready to resume all marital rights to his (often remarried) wife. Another frightening possibility was the affliction of lycanthropy, a dreaded condition which caused humans to act much like wolves. Today it is thought that this rare behavior may be a severe form of autism, as seen in a child who hates to be touched or looked at, and finds howling and growling far easier than speech. (The term derives from the Greek king Lycaon, who was changed into a wolf as punishment for serving Zeus human flesh when the god was his guest.) In the historical context of wolf-hating, however, it was easy to see a seemingly uncontrollable child as possessed by the vilest of animals.

Influenced by such tales, the arriving Europeans began ridding the land of both the wolves and the woods that had sheltered them. Armed with saws and mauls and axes and a hunger for enough fuel to warm their dangerously cold houses, they pushed the forests back so fast that by the mid-1700s New England was only about fifteen percent forested. For the next hundred years or so, the land was kept open, a naked topography except for the steepest of ravines and rocky hilltops. And when the hilltops became the wolf's last refuge, they too were cleared, as when Mt. Monadnock in southern New Hampshire was set ablaze, incinerating every animal driven up its sides. By the late nineteenth century, a recession had settled across the region; its soils were almost depleted, and the keeping of sheep was no longer profitable. Families abandoned their farms, walked away from their towns, and moved to the mill cities or to lands farther west.

In their wake, catkins drifted into meadows, birds scattered fruit, and the seeds of maple and pine blew across open ground. Soon acres of new trees grew out of the earlier remnants, and a sprawl of forest crossed the region again. Then these woods, too, were cleared in a second wave of cutting driven by an appetite for the pine used in all kinds of packaging. And when the advent of cardboard curtailed that demand (and mills in the South were able to supply cheaper pulp), this last reforestation took place, the one covering the hills around us now.

According to most estimates, only fifteen percent of New England is open land today, a complete reversal of the ratio a century ago. The habitat is ideal — because of the way we use it — for an animal able to exploit a patchwork shaped by our dependence on electricity and cars. Roads were cut through the woods, right-of-ways were cleared, houses were built on secluded, well-protected lots, and long lines of electricity kept everyone connected.

The coyote was quick to take advantage of the new maze of edges.

It loped into northern Vermont and New Hampshire in the early 1940s. It drifted into western Massachusetts and Connecticut about ten or so years later, about the same year I was born, when people were busy having babies and acquiring all the goods of the postwar prosperity. Few paid much attention to what slipped through the darker corridors, that new presence in the cornfield, something bigger than a fox in the cow pasture, a longish shape in the shadows where the garbage cans were stored. Then, in 1957, one was shot in Otis, a small town west of here, and the next year several were trapped near Massachusetts' Quabbin Reservoir. Coyotes had come to the neighborhood, or so a growing number of people were choosing to call the new animals.

They based their claims on the pattern of sightings, which began in southeastern Ontario in 1920 and moved to southern Quebec by the mid-forties. By the mid-fifties, the coyote was considered common in the Adirondacks. It took a few decades longer to reach the Canadian Maritimes, but the journey eastward persisted, with coyotes arriving in New Brunswick and Nova Scotia by the mid-seventies, and on Prince Edward Island and Newfoundland ten years later, presumably reaching both islands by crossing on winter ice.

It's an incredible trajectory, from the western plains to the Atlantic, all in less than a hundred years. It's a journey with so many clear markers, so many eyewitness accounts coming from farther and farther east, along with furs or photographs of shot or trapped animals, that it's hard to believe some people persisted in thinking that these animals were "escapees." Charles Cadieux, a government coyote control expert, insisted as late as 1983 that "tourists taking home coyote pups as pets have introduced these adaptable coyotes to the eastern U.S." And while it's true that a few caged coyotes were let loose (mostly from Army bases, according to a state wildlife biologist, where bored soldiers had kept them as pets until they grew too dangerous or expensive to feed), and a few more were released by sportsmen who thought the fast animals would be fun to hunt, the great majority arrived as part of a state-by-state, mile-by-mile expansion.

The new creature was clearly a coyote, or so went the prevailing wisdom, the same animal that could be seen in New Mexico or Arizona. According to Larry Pringle in a 1959 article in *Massachusetts Wildlife*, one had only to see its coloring ("tawny-gray, with black-tipped hairs"), find its track ("longer and more pointed than those of the average dog"), watch it eat ("venison, meadow mice or raspberries"), or hear its cry ("the well-known series of barks, ending in a long, quavering howl") to know that all the evidence was consistent with what was known about coyotes.

Fifteen years later, however, such confidence about its identity had begun to waver. There were too many uncoyote-like things about it, and there were no easy explanations for these deviations from type. One study found that the newcomer's feet didn't sweat, which made it more like a wolf than a coyote. Other studies found it was just a few pounds too large to fit into a tidy coyote category. In an oft-cited study comparing the skulls of various canids — wolves, domestic dogs, "coy-dogs," and the new arrival — a team of Harvard researchers found that this new animal's skull was consistently larger than a western coyote's. Yet it wasn't as large as that of a wolf.

What it *was* began to seem uncertain, and a growing discomfort was felt about its relatively large size; yet the feelings it provoked were immediate and palpable. When a fifty-pound male coyote was shot in 1972 in north-central Maine, dozens of people drove down miles of backroads to see it, "like primitive villagers gathered around the carcass of a man-eating tiger," according to John Cole, a *Maine Times* editor. "Hanging gaunt and stiff like a large gray dog, the animal hardly seemed awesome enough to warrant the mob hatred it seemed to engender." At about the same time, however, and also in Maine, biologist Daniel Hartman experienced the opposite reaction. His letter to the editor described a distinct joy when first hearing the new animal's howl. "I was shaking," he wrote, "elated. We have a new and noble predator in our state."

In Massachusetts, Raymond Coppinger, a professor at Hampshire College, undertook a study of the new canid with a team of his students, putting out a call for carcasses and roadkill. They published their findings the same year I finished high school. It's a "new wolf," they wrote in an article in *Massachusetts Wildlife*, "a new animal . . . brand new, our own, and not to be confused with anybody else's wolves or coyotes or wild dogs. Right here in New England, in the last half of the 20th century, a new animal has arrived, wolf-like in appearance, and it is found nowhere else in the world."

It was a fantastic notion, an idea so big it could change the way we thought about everything. Evolution was, after all, not something we were supposed to see within a lifetime, at least not the way Darwin had theorized it. Evolution, in his grand view, took place so slowly that not only could he not see it, neither could any of his peers, nor those searching for proof in the decades that followed. Evolution happened incrementally, over thousands of generations, a few chance variations through the long process of natural selection — longer ears, a thinner nose, a more highly developed sense of smell — all helping increase a species' chances of survival.

That was the theoretical construct I grew up with, as much a part of the landscape as the dinosaur tracks found along the Connecticut River and the horsetails that lined its incoming rills, thin plants barely changed in over 300 million years (other than to shrink in size from thirty feet to ten or so inches). The only real difference between Darwin's and our perceptions was that we viewed his idea matter-of-factly, while he comprehended its implications with terror (that evolution could create something as specialized as an *eye* made him "cold all over," while "the sight of a feather in a peacock's tail," he wrote a friend, "makes me sick!"). To those of us living a century and more later, evolution made total sense; organisms mutated and passed on the changed genes; the successful ones persisted and the tree of life kept branching, becoming more and more complex.

Yet the prospect of a new mammal arising from the land — within our lifetime — infused me with an edgy excitement at the possibility of what else might appear. I felt as shaken and elated as when Daniel Hartman first heard its howl. Large animals were not supposed to change in visible ways in so short a time. They were supposed to be as fixed in their shapes as were the creatures in Aesop's fables, unchanged since the last glacier scraped over the land — the Wolf, the Lamb, the Lion, and the Mouse. The animals we grew up with were so well-known in their habits that calendars could be composed of their comings and goings — the February day when skunks start to mate, the March moment when chipmunks emerge from their burrows, the nights in May when deer begin dropping their fawns.

And though there is some variation with every living thing — as anyone knows who has tried to match a bird in the bush with one in the book — none of it seemed as startling as this, as revolutionary as having a new animal in our midst. I loved all that the idea contained; it made the world seem larger.

Before the theory could take hold, however, another theory had to be debunked. For while the idea of a New Wolf was taking shape, so was the belief that it was simply a "coy-dog." The animals are produced, these advocates insisted, when dogs and coyotes mate. Thus their irregular size and their prevalence.

It's a myth that won't disappear, despite years of evidence to the contrary. Several times since returning I've heard people talk about the coy-dogs they have seen or heard, the packs of them traveling these hillsides. It's a misnomer that must linger because it's a less frightening idea than that of a *new and wild species* in our very backyards. Several studies had to be completed before this hybrid form could be discounted, however, the longest and best-known being that of biologists Helenette and Walter Silver, working in New Hampshire with National Science Foundation support.

Beginning in 1960 with five wild canid pups, the Silvers raised fifty-five animals from seven subsequent litters. They then bred one of the females with two different domestic dogs, and then cross-bred the young to obtain second-generation hybrids. At the same time, they began raising western coyotes imported from Colorado and Wisconsin as a way to compare behavioral traits among the various offspring. What they discovered from their original fifty-plus animals was what had been postulated all along: the "New Hampshire canid," as it had first been called, acted in most ways like a western coyote. Like wolves and coyotes everywhere, it had but one breeding cycle a year (domestic dogs have two), which took place in late January or early February.

The other animal they were raising, the coyote-dog hybrid, also had a single breeding cycle, but it occurred three to four months earlier than the coyote's. So though it was possible for a male dog to mate with a female coyote, the offspring of such a union would have to revert to the world of dogs, because no female coyotes would be in estrus in November, and male coyotes weren't physically available then. (The testicles of coyotes and wolves descend for only a few weeks a year to coincide with the female's availability.) A hybrid might mate with another hybrid, but the young kept reverting in type to coyote, throwing off the timing of estrous cycles. Another factor shedding doubt on the coydog theory was that the hybrid pups were born during January and February, the coldest, most difficult weeks of the year, when the parents would have to wade through deep snow to find enough food to sustain them. Actually, make that one parent — the father of said litter, like male dogs in general, assumes little or no responsibility for the feeding and care of the newborns.

The new canid, the Silvers concluded, should be considered a subspecies of the coyote, *Canis latrans*, and should be designated the "eastern coyote," *Canis latrans* var. Their study couldn't quite account for the differences within this coyote family — the larger size, the curious lack of foot sweat. Nor could they fully explain characteristics that were more typical of wolves than of coyotes; the eastern coyote was quite sociable and less inclined to be aggressive toward its siblings or its mate. These pieces of the puzzle they left for someone else to sort out.

Before the Silvers' findings were widely known, a bounty was established in New Hampshire on both the "timber wolf" and the "prairie wolf," for surely, went the belief in 1961, the new canid had to be one or the other. Four years later, with far more dogs shot than wolves and still no change in the coyote population, the bounty was dropped. Elsewhere in the Northeast, however, anger and confusion persisted, with anti-coyote sentiments gaining particular momentum in Maine. Though Maine's Division of Wildlife Services came out against introducing a bounty, insisting that nowhere had such a system kept the animals in check, legislation was introduced that would pay $50 per dead coyote. The representative who introduced the bill was adamant about the effectiveness of paying out money to obtain a goal. "I know for a fact that [bounties] worked pretty well here in York County, when the British were paying $50 a pair for Indian ears."

AMIDST ALL THE CONTROVERSY about its identity — new wolf or coy-wolf, coy-dog or western coyote — the animal itself kept on multiplying. So did the ways of responding to it — with awe, with hate, with a camera or a gun, with poisoned bait or a steel leghold trap. Evidence continued to favor the "coyote" des-

ignation, though, enough to prove useful in aiding its survival in the east. That it was not thought to be a wolf, at least in the 1970s, meant it was unlikely to prey on deer, and this gave hunters less reason to worry about competition. The various studies done on stomach contents, including one by Ray Coppinger's Hampshire College team, found that mice and rabbits made up a substantial part of a coyote's diet, their hair and bones found alongside pebbles, pine needles, grass, twigs, porcupine quills, apple seeds, fowl bone, tinfoil, and pieces of such trash as rope netting. It was clearly an opportunistic predator, they concluded, a calculating consumer unwilling to waste energy on hard-to-catch food. To one of these animals, a garbage pile was more attractive than a deer, and the ripe fruit in an orchard looked heaps easier to snack on than a flock of riled sheep.

By February 1975, agreement was finally reached at the annual Northeast Wildlife Conference, with conclusions much like those of Helenette and Walter Silver. This was a coyote, an "eastern coyote," an animal whose predecessors had spread north and east from its original home in the Southwest. (A separate wave of coyotes colonized the Southeast, with the Ohio River valley generally seen as the boundary between these two fronts. Much of this saturation took place in the sixties — several decades later than in the Northeast.) According to the thesis accepted in 1975, some of the animals taking the northern route had to have mated with the last gray wolves in Minnesota or the survivors that lingered on Ontario's southern edge, an exchange of genetic material that explained the new animal's large size. And then it kept advancing in a long trek eastward, a month-by-month, year-by-year journey, like a wave of immigrants driven from their homeland by drought or hard times, or like one of those other waves — of prospectors sure there's more gold in the hills, of carpetbaggers elbowing in after new money.

THAT WAS THE coyote's story as I understood it twenty years ago, and then I turned my attention to other things. But the controversies didn't end in the subsequent decades; they simply became more muted. It took returning to this area for me to hear them again; it took looking for some of the answers to realize how little is still known about coyotes and our respective relationships.

Now, as I scan the field, there's a good chance that ears will take shape between the steeplebush and maple saplings, along with a narrow, pointed muzzle, yellow eyes, and thin legs. With patience I'll see a certain heft to the shadows and soon that distinctive, German-shepherd coloring; or, better yet, it will appear in its startling blond or black phase. Whatever its color, I want to see it and think, *Wolf*, and then know it's a coyote, the species testing our boundaries in a way its larger cousin could not, an animal we haven't yet integrated into our collective imagination. Though the various western associations still linger — the slinking, trashy, mangy, nasty animals of the cartoons, the Wild West shows, the cowboy tales — this is a different animal, and I want to know how long it will take us to create a species-specific repertoire for this mix of wolf and coyote, old and new, necessary and fierce and wily.

"THEY'VE ALWAYS BEEN HERE," a naturalist tells me after we have been here a few months. He's been thinking about this theory for years, and he takes pleasure in startling people with it. "The coyote isn't a new animal at all," he says. "It's what the early colonists called a 'brush wolf.' They made a clear distinction between it and the gray wolf." The larger wolf was driven out, he believes, but the brush wolf wasn't, and it survived in those spruce-fir pockets that the big land clearings skipped, managing to hold on until the time was finally ripe for its successful reappearance.

But if it's a wolf, I ask him, where did it pick up its coyote DNA?

"It was there all along," he says. "The North American population of wolves and coyotes have always had some overlap. And those Indian fire pits excavated just east of here? They contained coyote bones. The only way they could have gotten there is if the animals were already present in the landscape."

I find additional support for his idea in an article by Ben Tullar, a wildlife biologist in upstate New York who insists that back in 1770 coyotes were as plentiful as they are today and that our forefathers simply didn't make a distinction between coyotes and wolves.

But surely, I think, an animal living in such pinched circumstances — hiding for decades in a few acres of swamp — would have evolved into something far smaller, a species putting all its energy into invisibility and fine-tuning escape. The eastern coyote is far bigger and more insouciant than that, a wonderful reversal of the trend toward disappearance (as many as 99 percent of once-present life forms are now believed to be extinct). In Massachusetts, for example, its numbers have leapt from some 500 animals in 1970 to anywhere from 3,000 to 5,000 today, though that is, of course, purely an estimate, which jittery wildlife officials are reluctant to give for a species that provokes such concern. In New York, which is six times the size of Massachusetts, the estimated population is six times as large as ours, or somewhere between 15,000 and 30,000 coyotes. In Maine, the current numbers are 10,000–16,000; in Vermont, there might be 1,200–2,000 in winter, with a post-whelping high of closer to 4,500.

In the past two months, I have seen three dead coyotes within fifteen miles of each other, all of them struck by cars. If each represented a pup from this spring's litters, that's a lot of coyotes being raised in this area. A population of 5,000 seems reasonable, a number amounting to one to two coyotes for every square mile. And that, to me, is an animal on a roll, infused with all the best of its sturdy wolf cousin, with *survivor* etched deep into each gene.

"We've had reports of coyotes on the campus of Northeastern University," Tom French of MassWildlife tells me, "of a coyote walking through a toll booth on a highway outside Boston, of a coyote crossing the Sagamore Bridge at two A.M. on its way to Cape Cod." They're in every state except Hawaii, finding dens in all kind of habitats — abandoned cars, tool sheds, Central Park, summer porches. They've wandered south as far as the Panama Canal and to all but the northernmost portions of Canada.

Their North American range is now larger than that of any other wild animal, and, by all accounts, they're spreading still.

COYOTES ARE AN ASSET, say some of the people I meet when buying four apple saplings, the first investment I make in our small plot of land. And they're arriving just in time. Just look at how many mice they eat, how many garden-destroying woodchucks and rabbits and grasshoppers.

They can't be trusted, say others, not with all that wolf influence in their blood. You can't be sure when they're going to realize that humans are easy prey, especially the toddlers that put up little resistance and offer plenty of soft flesh.

I sense the quiet shiver and remember the Ernest Thompson Seton story I read as a child, about a hunter in pursuit of a white wolf, a man obsessed with the animal that kept outsmarting him, a Captain Ahab of the desert Southwest. Wolves circled my room for nights afterward, and I had to seek refuge in the safety of my parents' bed, though even under their covers it was hard to escape the fierce howling in my head.

I suspect that if I were to read Seton's story now, I'd see the eroticism of it, the perverse intimacy with a prey both loathed and lusted after. The hatred in those tales surprises me still, a fury usually reserved for bitter enemies, for traitors, for those refusing to be crushed by Jim Crow laws or mob-driven lynchings. The lust is somewhat harder to pin down, the obsession prompting a hunter to learn everything he could about a single animal, sometimes spending more years tracking one wolf than in the company of another human being.

If at last he caught it, the ends had to be as difficult and emotional as the means, unleashing the same intense feelings of the hunt, of being humiliated by a four-footed beast.

Some bounty hunters were known to wire shut the jaws of a trapped wolf and leave it to the slow mutilation of dogs and insects. Some tied a wolf by its feet to nervous horses, sliced a line up its belly, then whipped the horses into quartering the body.

Some strapped a leather muzzle to a wolf whose legs were pinned in traps, then shot the animal in a slow pattern from haunches to heart until the ammunition and the fear were temporarily spent.

"MORE THAN ANY OTHER ANIMAL," writes Linda Hogan, wolves "mirror back to us the predators we pretend not to be, and

[thus] we have assigned to them a special association with evil." Fortunately, not only are coyotes smaller than wolves, but they run with their tails down, a look more submissive than the arrogant ride of their cousins. And though in regions such as Texas they may share the wolf's place as most reviled, they have been spared the more demonic associations, tweaking souls without totally terrifying them.

In the Native American myths where they figure most strongly, Coyote is the trickster, associated with bedevilment and inappropriate laughter, the rogue dancing on the periphery while pointing toes at our nakedness and bumbling. Coyote is the imp making us fart or trip when we're keenest to impress, causing us to drop the prized goods overboard, to set our own homes on fire, to show up in the wrong bed, the wrong clothes, the wrong life.

Even at the wrong theater, as in the performance I saw years ago by a group from Alaska, a fast-paced production that caught some of the more formal supporters of the new Maine Center for the Arts by surprise. Tuxedoed musicians accompanied coyote narratives, most of them gleaned from tribes in the Northwest. But the center almost lost its funding, and the director his job, after the troupe's outrageous enactment of "Coyote Breaks Wind."

It seems fitting that the coyote is the one species to have resisted the great westward push and turned east, filling the continent on either side of the Mississippi, the sole predator with the tricks and genes necessary to hold its own in our midst.

3

ON MY WAY to the community college, where I found a teaching job this fall, I pass an old house and wonder how long the walls can hold before the bittersweet vines that encircle it begin popping off shingles and slipping through windows. It's hard to imagine that someone could still occupy the slow-sagging house, but one day I saw a fox watching the building, its head cocked as though listening to someone shuffling about inside. Since then I have paid more attention as I pass, a quick glance from the fast-trafficked road. It's a way to keep adding to the story I'm inventing, in which the resident finds joy in the leaves' slow turn to red and in the way the sheltering vines embrace the dark building.

Although it's a recent arrival, bittersweet has already shrouded the native vegetation. The turkey vulture floating into sight above the ridge, large and dark against the thin wisps of cloud, is new, too; so is the purple loosestrife in the nearby pond, a few stalks still in bloom between stiff brown cattails. All three were inching into the landscape when I was small and learning the names of things, when cardinals and titmice were rare winter visitors, and house finches hadn't yet usurped so many backyard bird feeders. Today each newcomer is a reminder that change is continuous, that change is the one thing I can count on.

It's an emphasis I carry with me as I enter the school, where the new mandate for community colleges, the institutions that represent all that's egalitarian about higher education, is offering "remedial" classes as a way to make up for what public schools haven't done. In one such class this semester — Developmental

Reading — I find the gamut of abilities quite startling. For a few older students, this is the testing ground, the class that proves they're college material after all, that all the on-the-job problem-solving they have done over the years — figuring out insurances and mortgages and their children's homework — has prepared them well, and their delight is palpable. For the non-native speakers who simply need more practice in English — two students from the Ukraine, two from Japan, one from Tibet — the time feels similarly beneficial. But then there are the five who don't seem to understand what they read. They can't locate a thesis. They can't see that some details carry more weight than others. Metaphors escape them, as do irony, sarcasm, parody.

I'm sure that at some level they know they're reading for meaning all the time, at least in terms of physical details. That whenever they assess a person through the clothes he wears, the car he drives, or the music that spills from his headphones, whenever they take in the tattoos or tongue stud or nose rings, they're making meaning out of what they see. Each time they enter a bar, a club, a new apartment, the woods, they're engaged in the vital act of *reading;* they're taking in clues and figuring out whether they are safe there or not. But my analogies don't hold. When exploring a text, they don't sense the transferable skills, they can't find the written equivalents of piercings or jewelry or rhythms that sound familiar.

Our current essay, Scott Russell Sanders's "The Men We Carry in Our Minds," causes their eyes to glaze over. They don't understand why he would choose to write about men who labored hard or fought and died in wars, all the men from his childhood seen as either toilers or warriors. No connection stands out for these students between the oppression of laborers and the gains of the upper class. Nor will they speak critically of such people — "the big wheels of the big cities." They share too many of the same desires as the men Sanders criticizes. The career goals of these students are quite simple. "I plan to earn a lot of money." They can't tell me anything more specific about their interests or skills, about following a passion or someone they admire. The best job is defined simply by the size of the take-home pay.

None of the five of them lingers after class.

At home I circle the yard, I scuff leaves. I doubt I'll make any difference in their lives. I try to remember what brought me back here, and how changes in the cultural landscape made returning seem possible. And then I see the ladybugs, a swarm on the side of the house, large flocks on the studio walls, a shirr and busyness of insects touching down on my arms, my shoulders — more lady-bugs in one hour than I have seen in my lifetime. Inside, I find them pouring through cracks I hadn't known existed. They cluster high in the corners of every room; they arrive as though some dam has been rent, loosing a flood of bugs into the valley.

Turning away from the invasion, I put on an old shirt and head for the woods to look for the young buck I watched a few weeks ago. I want to find it alive and well, not the deer whose sev-ered head appeared in the street last week, its spike horns the same size as those of the animal I had seen. A set of ribs showed up next, a tangle of bones on the lawn of the red dog that's never leashed. In the days since, the skull has shifted from side to side in the road, in a different place each time I pick up mail from the box or drive past on my way to town. Cars skim it, the dogs toss it; so far no one has been moved to bury it.

I walk in the opposite direction from the road, watching for deer track in the soft earth near the brook, for signs of fur or bro-ken twigs. But before I enter the old apple orchard, grown thick with young hardwoods, I find a message so clear that a laugh slips from me. Coyotes have been here, and they have left scat at the very edge of the woods in the center of the path, a place impossi-ble to miss. I scan the woods; I squat down beside it and feel a con-versation beginning to take place.

With a jackknife, I push chunks apart, finding mostly hair and black cherry seeds. I slice deeper and find embedded clumps of fur, and a sight that ratchets up the tension between me and the world of the wild — four cat claws, nacreous as pearls.

LATE FALL HAS ARRIVED, the season of revelation. Trees stand stripped of their leaves, exposing hillsides, valley floors, backyards, bedroom windows. On our knoll I feel exposed, flushed from cover, not quite ready to admit, *I've come back, I've brought my lover.* We're careful with our language when speaking with my grandparents, with new neighbors, with old friends of the family. We laugh when we hear ourselves described as *the girls, the aunts, the women on the hill.* We hold back our impatience when people call one of us by the other's name, a common experience for same-sex couples.

I find myself trying almost daily to shed the image I'm sure must live on here, from when I was one of six kids, a staggered line of towheads, physically rowdy, verbally quiet, the spotlight on us too often because our father owned a large retail store that served as a hub in a mired and sleepy town. On some days, going forth into familiar places requires a conscious shoring-up, though the speed of the flashbacks still catches me by surprise. On Election Day, I give my name to the ballot clerk, and she exclaims, "I thought you looked familiar! You're finally back from the Appalachian Trail!" And then we both laugh, because of course I returned years ago, but stayed only long enough to catch the shocked reaction when I fell in love and knew for certain I had to leave again.

Yet I like being remembered; I like having an answer to the questions so often put to me in rural places — *Who's your family? Where are your people?* I like settling in a place where my roots go deep.

Tonight that pleasure grounds me as I stand under a sky rife with stars. Several jets course overhead, and I feel as much as hear the hum from trucks and cars on the distant Mohawk Trail. I watch for a shooting star, a flash of northern lights. Orion looms large as it lifts from the horizon, while above the Milky Way thickens.

Through air markedly softer and colder than the day's, I wade into the dark, knowing that this is the element I'll have to frequent more often if I'm going to see the coyotes that traverse this land. Nighttime is when most animals travel, and most of them I miss. It's also when birds travel farthest during migration. Some of that evidence is collected at dawn, when dead songbirds are shoveled off city streets, having collided with towers and skyscrapers overnight. And it's morning when I discover signs of some of the other travelers — the pocked lawn left by a skunk scrabbling for grubs and beetles, the hand prints on the compost bin marking a raccoon's attempts to get in, the owl pellet under the pines that contains bones of the night's take of mice.

In this dark I have to walk by feel, sensing the way as though blindfolded, expecting my skin to see the trees and low limbs and spider webs in front of me. It reminds me of the summer I spent every night outside, when I was hired to be the night watch at a craft school on Deer Isle, the responsible one who wandered between studios until the last artists went to bed and who stayed awake and watched the lobster boats heading out at dawn. I learned about night then — about the way foxes talk and raccoons argue, about the pulse and color of the aurora borealis, about the circling of constellations around the North Star, and about the way lovers, convinced of the secrecy of their affairs, give every detail away with the hungry sounds of their bodies.

It was also a job that rocked my interior clock, and I never quite learned when to catch up on sleep. Coyotes, on the other hand, though crepuscular, can sleep either day or night, depending on how weary or full they are and how close the perceived dangers lie. It's during denning season, however, the months of April, May, and June, when they're most likely to be observed during daylight. Not only do they need to keep watch over their pups, they need to supply them with a steady source of regurgitated food.

It takes about forty-five minutes for a human's pupils to fully adjust to the dark; it's only then that I can see almost as well as a coyote. But I'll never hear or smell as well as they can, nor sense through that combination of habit and expectation what's rustling the leaves, brushing pine needles, or pausing to lap at the brook. It has taken me hours to figure out that the scratching sound on the ground is that of worms excreting small castings, that the grinding sound in a downed pine comes from sawyer beetles making sawdust, that the patter on leaves, which can sound so much like rain, is actually the steady fall of caterpillar dung.

Tonight every noise seems sharply defined, each vibrating sound wave held longer than usual by the dampness of the night air. In this slow quiet, I like thinking that night does not *fall*, just as the sun does not rise or set. The turning of the planet causes darkness to appear — beginning in the lowlands, then dimming on the slopes, and at last winking closed on the highest summits. It's that rising I feel now, a lightening, as though I could travel easily and far through this dark in a kind of inward journey, covering very little ground while experiencing lots of internal energy.

I sense something in the woods, an animal that has also sensed me, and I scarcely breathe, hoping for coyote sounds, for the start of a wail, the first "Ow-ow-ow" that invites others to join in, that indicates the family is all around me, the same coyotes that called me from sleep that first night.

But the sudden, quick cry I hear is that of a fox, perhaps fifty feet away, a single soulful yip that speeds up my heart and that she repeats a minute later from farther down the trail.

4

CAPE COD, JULY 1998: A three-year-old boy is attacked in his backyard by a coyote. Driven by adrenaline, his mother beats the animal off, rushes the boy into the house, then repeats the frenzied defense when the coyote turns on her five-year-old daughter. Police shoot the coyote an hour or so later, but the impact of that struggle — a mother wild to keep an animal from dragging off her wounded child — lasts far longer in the community's consciousness. An autopsy on the animal can't explain the seemingly aberrant behavior. The coyote had had a broken leg, but it was fully healed, and there were no signs of rabies or distemper. There were numerous scars on its lungs from infection or worms, but that's typical of many wild canids.

It was the first direct assault of a coyote on a human in Massachusetts, though more than fifty similar attacks (including the killing of another three-year-old boy) have occurred in recent years in California, and there have been additional such instances in Arizona, Wyoming, Vermont, New Hampshire, and five Canadian provinces. The one consistent detail: most of the reports are of coyotes going after small children.

Such assaults will only escalate, wildlife officials tell us, as these opportunistic feeders learn to associate humans with easy meals. Coyotes already know that one of their preferred foods — domestic cats — can be found where people live; so can the easy pickings from garbage cans and compost heaps, county dumps and recycling stations. Coyotes will help themselves to pet dishes on the porch, ripe melons in the garden, the bag of fruit left overnight on the back steps. And the more they're rewarded for stalk-

ing suburban neighborhoods — ample calories with hardly any
expenditure of energy — the more their raids and numbers will
increase.

One animal control officer goes so far as to caution parents against letting small children walk unattended near woods;
they're too close in size, he says, to typical coyote prey. Others in
his position sound similar warnings, some voiced at a particularly
high pitch in articles such as "The Coyote 'Was Going for Their
Throats'" (*Arizona Daily Star*) and "Preying on People," from a
1999 issue of *Outdoor Life*, in which author Frank Miniter uses
some form of the word "blood" (bloody, bloodied, bloodcurdling,
blood bath, blood trail, dripping blood) almost as often as he does
the word "coyote."

Meanwhile, for the third straight year, a sharpshooter is
brought in to kill the coyotes who have swum to the Monomoy
National Wildlife Refuge, an island off Cape Cod that is a nesting
site for roseate terns and piping plovers, both of which are feder-
ally protected species. Despite loud opposition, the Fish & Wildlife Service managers believe it's their responsibility to protect the
small birds from predation by coyotes, and for $5,000 they hire a
gunman. He arrives with dogs, which lead him immediately to the
den and the ten healthy pups. It doesn't take long to dig into the
sand and shoot each one in the head.

"Monomoy is not a refuge for wildlife," claims a spokes-
woman for the local humane society. "When the refuge deliberately waits for the birth of pups and then kills the entire litter, it is
beyond logic." It's also a matter of conflict within the wildlife service: a biologist I spoke with on Plum Island, on the northern
coast of Massachusetts, said he didn't think the tiny plover chicks
would even register on the coyotes' radar. There's plenty of other
food available to them, he said, like fawns and dead fish and picnic
scraps the gulls haven't finished. Others point out that the sea
edge is such a productive place to live that coyotes will keep trying

to colonize the island, that there's no way of stopping their desire for an empty niche.

In the articles I've begun gathering, I find a University of Massachusetts survey that polled people on whether they favored legal protection or additional control measures for coyotes. The results were inconclusive. Despite the frequent mention of coyotes in the news, despite the increased number of howls heard in towns — triggered by sirens, train whistles, loud music, or barking dogs — and despite the unexplained dashes of gray across highways, only about 20 percent of the respondents report ever having seen a coyote, and 51 percent feel they don't know enough to answer the questions. One focus of the study, however — the "existence value" of coyotes — makes my jaw tighten; the phrase triggers an image of the great Chain of Being, an elaborate hierarchy that placed Europeans in charge of ranking the worth of every other living thing.

An equally provocative phrase — "cultural carrying capacity" — is used to identify collective tolerance levels, in this case of the number of coyotes people will accept in their neighborhoods before they register discomfort. Given the volume of complaints that animal control officers and wildlife officials have fielded over the past few years, these specialists suggest we may have reached that capacity. I feel weighed down by this approach to wildlife, by the idea of making decisions based on easily manipulated evidence. I see numbers pitted against numbers, no single perspective large enough to assess the myriad possibilities. "Cultural carrying capacity" captures us at our most primitive and reactionary, scared by the cluster of teenagers on the sidewalk, by the single mothers outside the welfare office, by people with AIDS taking to the street, fragile and hurting. The concept freezes us in time, without history or future, defenseless when presented the slick visuals of media campaigns. Give us an hour with Bambi or Smokey the Bear, with Hitchcock's *The Birds*, and we're caught in a response controlled by someone else, an emotional roil as likely to be driven by market forces as by politics or cultural mores.

It's not surprising that I want to hear the snarl and see the teeth of a coyote, that I want to turn a corner and find one there, facing me, so that I can experience all that rises at the moment of encounter — fear, awe, or great gladness that such a resilient and large animal exists in the world. In the weeks or months before that happens, I want to feel shadowed by a presence that raises the hairs my neck, that leaves an odor I can't name, that deposits scat on the path and fades between trees, disappearing mere seconds before I look up.

I want to spend hours in the woods, as taut and cupped as an ear.

WE TAKE DIFFERENT PATHS to learn about this place where we live. Holly heads first to the local library, the coffee shops, the historical society, curious about the cultural life of the area, about the waves of immigrants that have passed through and the ones that have chosen to stay. I need to know the trees first, the birds and animals, and how the land has been used and what foods it produces. To answer the bigger questions about cycles and patterns, I head to the University of Massachusetts in Amherst. Here I retrace earlier steps, as though I might find in some old map or journal the lure that once drew me to the school and the subsequent discoveries that sent me reeling away.

In the government documents room on the sixth floor of the library, I locate the annual reports of the Massachusetts Division of Fisheries and Wildlife. In their pages I find a compressed history of the last few decades in language and images that I recognize. The early issues, from the 1950s to the 1970s, primarily contain lists of body counts and pelt prices, of the marketable surplus of muskrat and mink, of fox and deer, of quail and pheasant and salmon and trout. (A muskrat pelt in '55 is worth $1; in '66 it's up to $1.75. Mink prices take a small dive during the same years from

$18 to $9, while a beaver fur holds steady at $17.) There's little mention of any efforts by the state to restore fragile or dwindling populations, other than the plans to bring back wild turkeys and to establish flocks of resident Canada geese (regrettably successful). And no attempt is made to explain dramatic shifts in populations, such as the startling moment when fishers returned, their arrival noted only in the numbers trapped — two in '75, twenty-three in '76 — or when suddenly there were enough coyotes for trappers to earn good money.

The 1980s start with a similar emphasis on total harvests of deer and gamebirds and fish, along with the announcement of two new hunting seasons, one on turkeys and the other on coyotes. The inflection with each is the same as in the notice that the taking of frogs ("long a contentious issue") will no longer require a permit. The only exception to this emphasis on harvesting game is in the attention paid to the bald eagle and the piping plover, two precarious species newly aided by the state.

By the 1990s, all that has changed. Over half the annual report is now devoted to the status of threatened or endangered species — the common loon, the peregrine falcon, the Plymouth red-belly turtle. Coyotes appear now in two different categories — under total numbers hunted or trapped (which are no longer being tallied after the Wildlife Protection Act takes effect) and under that nebulous category of "animal complaints" (242 of the state's 351 cities and towns report coyote problems). The implicit theme of these later issues is that the department's revenue is no longer derived solely from the sale of fishing and hunting licenses. There is a new constituency now, made up of any taxpayer in the state who chooses to donate to the Endangered Wildlife Conservation Fund via his or her tax return.

It's a significant change, for not only has the department had to widen its focus, but the wider society has altered its perceptions as well. For the coyote, that means its arrival was perfectly timed, another factor in enhancing its chances of survival. Had it appeared any earlier, it might not have achieved such a level of health. But with protection and expansion on everyone's mind, the glory days for the new canid are now just beginning.

Still, I think, as I stack books on carts and gather my notes, most people don't know coyotes are around unless their cats disappear, their dogs won't stop barking, or another newspaper headline catches their attention. "Coyotes: A Howling Success." "Proliferation of Coyotes Concerns Police Chief." "Coyotes Among Us." "The Killer Controversy." Some still refuse to believe they have coyotes for neighbors until they hear a story like that of the coyote found inside a house in Hatfield, which entered through a basement window and wandered up the cellar stairs. The woman's cats knew something was there and wouldn't come home all weekend. The owner, however, didn't find out until early Monday morning when, waking up with coffee, she discovered the animal under the kitchen table. She started, it bolted, and she thought it had escaped out the door. But when she returned from work that afternoon, she entered a house heavy with the smell of a scared animal. A windowsill was chewed, a lamp broken, the carpet stained with urine and feces. She called the local animal control officer, who found the young female hiding in a closet. Even after being tranquilized, the animal managed to leave teeth marks on the pole he used to tote her away.

From one of the library's high windows I watch a swan on the campus pond turn ugly. It flails up the bank, wings out, neck down, intent on grabbing a backpack the owner is rushing to yank away. For a moment, it's Leda and the Swan, a stronger-than-plausible force that the young woman can't seem to influence. But she's no pliant maiden; she's stubborn and strong, and ultimately she wins the brief tussle.

The swan ruffles back to the center of the pond, and I opt for the many flights of stairs rather than the close confinement of the faster elevator.

5

"COYOTES ARE FRIGHTENING," says Diane, who looks unafraid of anything, especially now as she relates the story, a fresh scar across her throat from the surgical repair of a recent injury. "And they're incredibly active at night, when there are more of them out there than you could ever guess, and all of them running through the woods. So many animals at night, running through the woods."

She remembers the details as though it happened last week, not that November afternoon two years ago, with a bit of daylight remaining and the chance to spend a few hours deer hunting, a passion she discovered after marrying her second husband. ("Before Gene," she says, "I wore high heels and had hair out to here.") She picked an area a few miles from home that she knew well enough to try all alone. But she didn't bag the buck she was after, and when the shadows began to merge, darkness crowding up against her, she struggled to find the way back to her truck. Before she could get there, the coyotes began howling, coyotes all around her, howling despite her yells or the rapid shots she fired.

Had there been a moon, she might have made it out that night. Had she brought a flashlight, she might have been fine. And had she had a cell phone — she won't travel now without one — she could have made a call to her husband, to a friend, to one of her daughters, someone to please come find her, a human voice in the woods helping pin down her location, helping deflect the idea that the coyotes knew exactly where she was, the hunter become prey, the wild animals with all the advantage in the dark, when she couldn't make out anything familiar, least of all the stone wall she was supposed to cross to get back to the road.

She had nothing to keep the dark at bay except matches, and when the distances shrank too much to feel safe, she found a tree she knew she could climb. Then she started a small fire and fanned it hard, producing flames enough to light her way in finding more wood, branches she hauled close enough to be able to reach each time she descended in the night. Using the black plastic bag that was intended for deer guts, she fashioned herself a pullover to slow the loss of body heat and made her way up the tree. There she tied herself to the trunk, in case she nodded off to sleep, and listened to the coyotes, sensing them all through her body. She was never, she still claims, so terrified in all her life.

PRIOR TO DIANE'S STORY, I hadn't read or heard of adults being attacked by eastern coyotes, though there had been instances of people getting roughed up when the dog they were holding was grabbed or the kid they were protecting was rushed by an animal, resulting in puncture wounds, lacerations, some traumatized suburbanites and alarmed picnickers. But Diane knew what coyotes are capable of doing, at least to a weakened deer or soft fawn, and she was taking no chances while alone in the woods.

I've also never heard proof of a nonrabid wolf attacking a human, though wolf attacks are one of those hard-to-prove areas of local lore in which fact is usually impossible to separate from hearsay. Barry Lopez, in *Of Wolves and Men*, writes of several studies that tried to determine whether wolves did or did not see men as prey. In one, completed in 1945, the U.S. Fish and Wildlife Service reported that none of the incidents of wolf attacks over the previous twenty-five years could be substantiated. And when the editor of the *Daily Star* of Sault Ste. Marie, Ontario, offered $100 to anyone who could document such an attack, the reward money went uncollected.

But a powerful force continues to fuel the stories, the same thing that sent Diane up the tree in the first place — "Throw in a measure of fear," she says, "and there's no way to know what's really out there." It makes me wonder about the way we signal our dread, the way it seeps from us like a scent, a message that tells the coyote something about advantage, about who, at that moment, is in the better position.

Lopez and others see something similar in the wolves they watch, intimations that seem part of a bigger conversation. The wolves seem to catch a prey's "signal" that it is weak or wounded, a nervousness in marked contrast to the other members of the herd: "Prey animals such as these," Lopez writes, "apparently announce their poor condition to the wolf in the subtleties of a stance, a peculiarity of gait, a rankness of breath . . . It seems clear that prey selection is something [in which] both animals play a role."

I imagine that happens with coyotes as well; some twitch or restlessness is perceived in the prey, some sense of doom the compromised animal can't mask. I suspect that the peaceful scenes I've heard people describe, of cows and coyotes together in a field, the cows seemingly unperturbed by the coyotes' close presence, indicate that all were healthy animals with nothing to fear from each other. (Coyotes can, after all, kill healthy cows and goats and sheep, though the expense of energy is large, as is the risk of injury.) Had one of those cows shown, however, that some injury or infection had weakened it, then the coyote might have had to test that animal, forcing it to reveal whether it had strength enough to run or fight, or was so weak that the coyote had but to wait and the meal would be easy. And, surely, coyotes share that same stare of the wolves, that "exchange of information . . . that either triggers a chase or defuses the hunt right there," what Lopez calls "the conversation of death."

I have seen something similar among dogs, in two experiences memorable because they occurred so close in time to each other. The first involved a big German shepherd, owned by the woman, who was white, from whom I rented a room. Rip, who suffered badly from hip dysplasia, senility, and a terrible allergy to fleas, rarely moved faster than a stumble except when scratching his hot skin. Yet the day a black postal carrier hurried up the sidewalk, Rip was suddenly lunging at the man as though he would kill him, his barking and the man's yelling bringing Nancy and me out of the house. "It's embarrassing," Nancy said later, after we were all back inside, "but he just doesn't like black men."

The other dog, short-legged and part terrier, with a small dog's high yip, belonged to an African American friend with whom I was collaborating on a project. The UPS man was arriving one day when I stopped by, and Zora flew past me, heading for the man's thighs, groin, whatever she could reach. Monifa hurried to pull the dog back before Zora could do any damage, and then said matter-of-factly as we stepped into the house, "She doesn't like white men. She never has."

Though I respected the thinking of both of these women, I had a hard time believing their dogs could distinguish both sex and skin color and find the necessary matches, male and black, male and white. I suspected each responded to some silent emission of a deep and old fear, some signal that aroused a predator's fury within them.

THE QUESTION OF what triggers attack — "the conversation of death" — has haunted me since learning about the murder of a woman I had hiked with on the Appalachian Trail, and I never think of Jan without remembering every detail of those first days in Georgia, from the misery of sheeting cold rains to the delight of living on what I could carry on my back.

About a dozen people started the journey within a week or so of each other in early March, and we formed a close group, traveling together during the day, sharing shelters at night, all the while coping with mice in our packs, skunks on our beds, raccoons clever enough to open zippers and jars. One of the hikers had a dog, which required a whole different vigilance, particularly the night we used ponchos and tarps to barricade the lean-to from the lash of icy rain, yet somehow a spotted skunk was able to shimmy his way in. The dog caught its tail, Jan grabbed the dog, and miraculously in the melee none of us was sprayed.

But the lousy weather convinced Jan's traveling companion to quit, and then Jan had to decide whether to continue alone. She must have taken a few days off somewhere, because I got ahead of her in North Carolina and never saw her again.

I met Paul, the man who killed her, at a lean-to just south of the Virginia line. I think there were five of us hiking together then — Jim, Chris, Paula, Suzanne, me. I was wobbly and dehydrated from a bout with dysentery and wanted nothing more than to crawl into my sleeping bag and stay there for a day or two. But Paul was warming to the company; Paul was emptying his last tea bag into rolling paper to smoke, and in the pleasure of his voice I forgot my queasy innards.

He told us where to get good water and how to avoid the dogs that lived between the shelter and Damascus. He had been to the town a few times, he said, earning money when he could by pruning trees. He wore cowboy boots, had no teeth, and also had no food, which, when we realized it, had us parceling out what we could shave from our stashes — soup mix, raisins, cocoa, pasta — while he shared schemes and more stories.

He told us he had nine kids and a passel of grandbabies, and he couldn't stand life after his wife up and died. Someone told him about the Appalachian Trail, and the details were enough to convince him to catch a ride from Tucson to New Hampshire, where he found a trail marker and started walking south. (None of us said anything at the time, but his feet contradicted him, for no one hikes in cowboy boots; no one.) His real dream, though, was to travel with pack burros from Colorado to Alaska, a trip he thought might take two years. Tree work, again, would sustain him. Though — he mused, he smoked, he sampled a handful of someone's high-protein snack mix — he thought he might try prospecting, too, having spent seven years hunting for gold in the Superstition Mountains and another chunk of time stealing gold out of Mexico. At least that's what he called it — "stealing" — and while his shrug said it was easy, his face said that the fact of it still made him uncomfortable.

I fell asleep to the sound of his voice and felt safe and lulled and glad the world was big enough to include people like him. I didn't try to sort out what was truth and what was fiction in all he spilled, nor did the others as we continued north over the weeks and months, cooking and hiking and finding shelter together. Instead I held on to the image of his curious smile as he accepted our small offerings of food, of his blue nose, which looked as if it had been frostbitten more than once, and of his quiet pleasure in smoking tea leaves. Those scenes helped me resist the rumor I heard later, somewhere in Pennsylvania, that a man living in one of the shelters had thrown a hatchet across the campfire and killed a through-hiker from Wisconsin. I kept it distant, something someone must have misremembered after reading scraps from old newspapers, the stuff left behind in some itchy, hot laundromat.

And I was busy observing the ways people treated us, giving us rides to the nearest restaurant, grocery story, or post office, offering something unexpected — an orange, a can of tuna, a hot shower in a dry house. The accumulation of all those small gestures gave the hike its weight in my life: the single act of every person who held out a hand, a sack of cookies, a cold beer; who stopped a truck and let me throw my pack in back; who helped me find a doctor when tendonitis flared in my ankles, a telephone when I needed to call home, a safe place to stay when I couldn't get back to the trail before dark. Complete strangers helped me get a prescription filled, my camera repaired, a package mailed, and they directed me to the best all-you-can-eat buffets, to the YMCA ($2 to spend the night, $3 to use the laundry), and to the town hall, where through-hikers could sleep on the floor if no dances or other socials were scheduled for the evening.

I hope Jan met some of those people, too. I prefer not to imagine what else she encountered, especially that evening by the campfire when she must have suddenly felt afraid in the company of a man she wasn't sure about, her fear like that of prey.

The morning I parted company with Paul, the sunrise was dark red. A few miles later, I entered the post office in the tiny town of Damascus, relieved to find that my spare boots had arrived and that a kindly postal clerk would help me find enough packing material to ship my worn-out boots home.

A few days later, Paul walked into the same town and told them what he had done.

I HURRY into my brother's arms, liking the smell and strength of him, the unruly sprawl of his eyebrows, the trace of summer in his face and hair. I like the way his eyes light up when he sees me and how we move toward each other at the same time. And then it happens. We misjudge and hit too hard; we miss with our aim, and immediately we pull back, surprised yet again.

We shouldn't be. He's the only person I do this with, my brother Bob, who's only fourteen months older than I and about whom I will probably never have one single, uncomplicated feeling. We're both coordinated, fluid-moving people except for those first moments around each other when our faces should be able to brush against each other's and don't.

He asks how Holly and I are doing in the new house, if we've found anyone to plow our steep driveway, whether we'll be heating with wood this coming winter. He seems glad for the physical things I can do, though he's willing to wager that I've forgotten some of the difficulties of rural living in the north, and here we are without a four-wheel-drive vehicle, without a back-up heat source, with a long driveway and only two shovels. I'm sure a part of him suspects he'll have to rescue us from some storm or dilemma, some untoward event that would require his skills. I reassure him that we're doing fine and then, without intending to, I tell him about the coyote that has been crisscrossing our land, tell him I suspect that soon I will see it.

"Ha!" he says. "If I see a coyote, I'll shoot it. They kill cows. They kill sheep. They're nothing but trouble." He puffs up, a visible ratcheting of bravado, and I see again a photograph his ex-wife took when they were still married and my brother had just caught an opossum with his bare hands. In the photo, he holds it high by the scruff of its neck, the animal a sack at the end of his arm, both faces glaring at the camera. The looks are remarkably similar, each in a ferocious, teeth-bared snarl, both equally afraid and adrenaline-pumped and certain that the minute my brother lets go, there will be a confrontation, and it will be messy.

We separate into the big circle of family, and I repeat my message, this time with my sister Liza, though why this search matters is more than I can explain over a holiday get-together. "I want to see a coyote," I tell her.

She nods and tosses back her dark hair. "Come over to my house," she says. "I hear them all the time." Then she moves to greet Holly, which gives me more chance to watch her.

Liza's the smallest of the six of us and was once, perhaps, the bravest. She's also the most delicate in her features, the one people stopped to stare at — *she's so beautiful* — while the rest of us pretended not to care. I look like Bob, the same raw blond coloring, narrow face, and high cheeks, with a build similar enough to pass ourselves off as twins when we were little. But the two of them, Bob and Liza, are the closest in temperament. As kids, they were the hot bloods, each quick to anger, slamming doors or hurling whatever was within reach — alarm clocks, books, toys, chairs. Over the years, she cooled her temper down, her voice only occasionally giving away the underlying roil, the possibility that two messages would collide, two fuels would mix that shouldn't. Then, without warning, she might spiral into a swirl of laughter, outrage, weeping.

Bob's temper fires when we least expect it.

I help carry food. I share my parents' joy at gathering us all around the tables. I bask in the weave of voices, the many children, the good smells. The long eating is ended when the first shift begins washing dishes, and Bob starts a story about a recent trip with a friend of his, a man paralyzed from the waist down. The two have hunted together for years, traveling the back roads in his friend's specially equipped van. This time, however, they were only a few miles from home when a deer appeared at the side of the road. The friend didn't have time to grab his gun, so he tried to run down the deer with his van instead. My brother, laughing now at the absurdity of it, told his friend to head instead for a place where the road nears the river. Sure enough, the deer had raced down to cross there, and this time the driver was ready to take aim.

Some of us laugh with him, glad the end for the deer was fast and that the van-slamming technique wasn't tested. Glad, too, in some more necessary way, that Bob wasn't the one at the wheel, that he's some kind of stabilizing influence on his friend. None of us laughs at the idea contained in other stories, of guys poaching deer, or how it fits with Bob's belief in self-reliance — *You have to get your meat somewhere.*

The dishes done, the kids disappear outside, and the rest of us sprawl in the living room, overly full of Thanksgiving dinner. I watch Bob tell Holly another story, something about one of his kids, something he knows she'll understand because she too has a son who is easy with guns, and I walk to a window and look west to

the hills. Shooting didn't always have such a place in these stories, though I'm having a hard time separating what was part of
our childhood and what came about in the years we lived far from
each other. Shooting rats in the barn, chopping off snakes' heads,
blowing up the occasional frog with a cherry bomb — those were
childhood experiments, not knee-jerk reactions to the surprises
coming at him.

But then he was mugged one night in New York City — a
man rushed at him with a section of a two-by-four and he had
barely enough time to duck, the board catching him on the forehead instead of in the throat. In a fury, blood streaming into his
eyes, he retaliated, my tall, powerful brother, the one I competed
with until I was nine or ten, until the fist fight that made clear
he would always be stronger. As for the would-be mugger, my
brother left him in a heap on the sidewalk, maybe alive, maybe
dead, and went back to the hotel, his head swollen and pounding.
A few weeks later, when the fear and rage had started to abate, he
contacted an old friend, someone who knew someone who was a
police officer in the city. The man did some searching of the rec-
ords, but nobody had been found that night, in that spot, and that
was as far as they dared take their worry.

It's a story that shapes how I see him, how I think about the
randomness of violence and how easy it is to think of it as happening somewhere else — to my brother, to Jan on the Appalachian
Trail, almost to Diane as the coyotes circled her tree all night. It's
far more difficult to admit that I, too, may harbor it or be drawn to
it for reasons I can't explain. Yet it's that very possibility that Linda
Hogan brings home in "Deify the Wolf." In pursuing these large
mammals, she writes, "we are looking for the clue to a mystery, a
relative inside our own blood, an animal so equal to us that it re-
flects back what we hate and love about ourselves."

6

IT SNOWS AT LAST, fine, cold snow falling all afternoon and into the night, and at dawn I pull on layers of clothing and head out into the tail end of the storm. It's slow going, but not because of the eight inches of new powder. It's the wind that makes my eyes tear, driving loose snow from lingering flurries and freeing branches of their loads. I squint; I shelter my face. I see little that moves, other than a pair of juncoes under the shelter of hemlock boughs. No footprints appear anywhere on this crystalline cover; whatever else lives here won't venture forth until the storm is over and the winds abate.

The next morning I try again. The wind chill is close to −20° F; the bitter air amplifies sounds. Beech and oak leaves rattle on their stems; the wispy calls of brown creepers and kinglets sound high and fine between gusts. Birch catkins and the furred cones of sumac seem to have exploded as the temperature dropped, scattering red and brown seeds across the surface of the snow.

But the only tracks I see in the hours I wander are those of a gray squirrel. No fox, no grouse, no weasel, no mice. And, disappointingly, no coyote.

To find one, I'm beginning to realize, will require a strategy different than a reliance on chance. I'll need to depend on the same radar that allows me to see sand dollars, four-leafed clovers, and the eggs and young of luna moths. And owls, which one friend says must be my totems, though all I know is that sometimes I sense one nearby, and I go outside in the daytime and there it is, its eyes shut, its body still and pressed close to a tree trunk. Or something will pull me awake at night, I'll head out the door, and sure enough, a great horned owl hoots from deep inside the woods, or I'll stumble farther and there, by the brook, I'll find a saw-whet owl bathing in a still, moonlit pool.

I want a similar sixth sense to kick in and tell me a coyote is right here, right now, darkly outlined against the thick woods.

SIXTY YEARS AGO OR SO, when that lone coyote first smelled a wolf, her survival instinct should have been to flee, to run without ceasing, to find a cave too small or ice too thin for the larger wolf to follow and kill her. For some reason, however, she didn't escape. She may have tried but reacted too late, or the wolf was too strong, or they were simply too far from their social networks to do otherwise. Because what followed was not the attack that meant sure death to the coyote, but the roughing-up of foreplay, the hit-and-nip attention that signaled affection. It went on for several hours, maybe a few days, on a day that might have looked like this, in snow in late January, somewhere in Ontario or northern Minnesota.

The coyote was of average size and build; she was fast, though not especially so. What distinguished her from her littermates had been her aloofness. Of the lot of them, she was the one least interested in the return each day of her parents; she was the one most likely to be off exploring while her siblings busied themselves with bones and the tossing of dead mice. In the fall, she and a few other transients, one or two from distant litters, had begun scouting for open land with good prey and better cover. They found unmarked tracts as they pushed east and only occasionally the fresh scent post indicating the presence of a wolf.

The wolves, meanwhile, had been retreating to the north and west, almost gone from the lower forty-eight states (other than the few that remained around Lake Superior, on Isle Royale), pushing against those packs with territories in the provinces of

central Canada. This particular winter had found a few living alone, including the wolf who picked up the scent of a female coyote in estrus, and for him there were no other potential mates or rivals around. The other coyotes scattered; the wolf kept advancing. And then, in an act rare for mammals, which seldom interbreed, and in an even rarer act for wolves, whose packs have strict taboos against mating with outsiders, he chased her, he had to, struggling at first to keep up, but he was bigger and stronger and handled the drifts with greater ease. He tackled and pinned her; he held her ruff when she was back on her feet; he ran alongside her, then knocked her over; he pressed her flat and let her escape, every moment and movement giving each of them the chance to know the other's smells and strength and readiness.

Then he held her with his forelegs, pulled her back against

his belly, and did what all members of the dog family do. And maybe she didn't resist; maybe, despite all they understood about each other, they sensed this was mutually beneficial. Whatever instinct might have insisted, some other innate trigger won over, and he succeeded in mounting her. Then, carefully, he lifted off, his penis still inside her, and twisted around, their back legs almost touching, the two remaining tied, their hindquarters touching, for the thirty minutes or so the act of fertilization requires.

It's a terribly vulnerable position to be in, a half-hour spent facing away from each other, neither one able to run or scratch or lie down, yet all the while completely aware of the other and of their visibility, two dark animals against a field of white snow. It's a bizarre practice to have survived evolution's fine-tuning, though perhaps such a lengthy, risky ritual helps ensure that the couple will remain monogamous, the way sharing trauma can create unlikely bonds between all kinds of individuals.

The odds were definitely against this particular union. They had to find a den in this new territory, though the wolf might have had one already staked out. They had to accommodate different domestic preferences — coyotes like old woodchuck or fox dens, or rocky, sheltered crevices, while wolves prefer to excavate their own, with an entrance tunnel six to eight feet long and a large chamber dug at the end. But that was just the beginning of their many adaptations. The two didn't hunt the same way, their dietary needs weren't the same, and their experiences didn't quite mesh for the rending of meat. Yet they persisted. For nine weeks they traveled together, sharing food and shelter, warning each other of possible dangers. In early April, when the sun had softened the snowpack and a percussive melt fell around them, the female gave birth to five or six pups (four to six is average for wolves, five to seven for coyotes, though if it had been a good winter, with plenty of food for both of them, she might have whelped between ten and twelve pups, all blind and deaf and dependent).

That's the point at which there should have been others around to help out, the aunts and uncles of both species who stick around through the winter and spring, taking turns feeding and training the young and keeping them in line when the parents are away from the rendezvous sites. But this pair was alone; there were no other strong bodies to help bring down large game, so their diet consisted mostly of mice, hare, squirrels, and grouse until calves and fawns were born to the nearby moose and deer, which proved easy prey for the stronger wolf.

Thus tended, several of the young again beat the odds (about half of all wolf and coyote pups die in their first six months) and didn't succumb to the big killers of hypothermia, pneumonia, heartworm, and distemper. They ate well, played hard, learned to hunt, and lived into the fall. At that point, they could have stayed together, thereby increasing their chances of surviving another winter, or dispersed, coyotes with some wolf DNA, heading ever eastward. The going would be difficult. Ontario's bounty system was still in effect, as was the wolf war Canada was waging against this perceived enemy of caribou.

In the story I'm imagining, they lived together through one more season, and the following April the female delivered again. The one-year-olds helped with feeding and training the new littermates, a further mixing of behaviors from both of their gene pools. And that autumn, a few of the well-fortified older siblings headed off together, following the northern edge of the Great Lakes, intent on finding territory they could claim for their own, each animal a little stockier and stronger than the coyotes that had first made it to Canada.

OTHER THAN COLD, it's teaching that gives my days their definition, though the best exchange today happens not in the Women and Literature class, but afterward, in the hall, when two young women tell me about seeing the movie *Jane Eyre*, and I ask what they know about Charlotte Brontë. Though both are fairly conversant with contemporary culture, neither has ever heard of her. They think the movie sprang fully formed from a scriptwriter's mind; they hadn't imagined an author laboring one hundred fifty years earlier, shocking the world with her unregenerate Jane.

I want the writer to come alive for them. I want them to know how she and her siblings lived, and why she first published under a male pseudonym. I tell them that Charlotte Brontë based Jane Eyre's experiences on her own, when she and her older sisters were sent off to a school for the daughters of impoverished clergymen, where two of the sisters died from diseases they caught there. I tell them that Jane's love for Rochester was probably modeled on Charlotte's unrequited love for a married teacher she met at a school in Brussels. Then I list the sequence of events — how she became a literary phenomenon almost overnight, how her brother died, followed by her two remaining sisters. That left her father and the man she agreed to marry at the age of thirty-eight, and within a year she, too, was dead, from the complications of pregnancy.

They shudder at the grimness and at the same time are intrigued, so I tell them about the town of Haworth and the cemetery's location above the Brontë house. It's a perverse urge on my part, but it's one of the images I'll never forget from a trip I once made there. I want them to share my horror at the docent's theory about the slow leach of toxins from the graveyard into the water supply, a titrated dose to weaken each of the Brontës slowly.

"Gross," they say. "Gross."

I may have gone too far. "So what about that mad woman in the attic?" I ask.

Again one says, "Gross," and our time is over, they have to rush to their next class, and I step outside into the sting of winter.

I bet the gales across the moor felt far fiercer than the wind that now buffets my car. If so, it should have made them sturdier, Charlotte and her sisters, though each sip of water probably set them back at the same pace the wind advanced them, keeping them from ever achieving any real gains in hardiness.

Closer to home, I scan the edges of a cornfield, the scraped land under the power lines, the same sweeping look I make each time I drive this road. Nothing moves; nothing looks out of place, and I remember another detail from that trip to Haworth — a pair of Charlotte's shoes on display in a glass case. I was stunned by their tiny size — surely less than six inches — and could scarcely imagine a writer of her stature navigating the world on such puny pins. Though Charlotte Brontë was an exception ("her hands and feet were the smallest I ever saw," according to her biographer, Mrs. Gaskell), what stands out in equal measure is how much we have increased in size over the years. We're bigger on average than our Victorian counterparts; our skeletons are longer, as are our feet. It's a change that has even made the news of late, with pediatricians citing numerous examples of infants and toddlers that have completely outpaced all normal growth rates. The causes may seem obvious — better nutrition and prenatal care, perhaps even the possibility of supplemental growth hormones showing up in our food. Whatever the cause, the outcome is there, at least for North Americans. We're on the rise.

So are coyotes.

We're both bucking the trend, in geologic time anyway, toward a reduction in size. The reasons vary from shifts in climate and habitat to changes in predator-prey relationships, with the overall pattern following a long, downward arc. We know from fossil evidence that most dinosaurs dwarfed the reptiles of today, that at least one dragonfly had a two-foot wingspan, and that a condor-like species had a wingspan stretching twenty-five feet — more than twice as wide as that of the wandering albatross, which casts the widest shadow of any bird alive today.

Of course, the very first mammals were probably mouse-sized insect eaters, but the creatures that evolved after them make today's relatives look minuscule. Some of the fossils from the La Brea Tar Pits in southern California include a lion bigger than any of today's descendants, an enormous short-faced bear, a bison with horns six feet long, and three species of massive ground sloths. In the eras since, mammals slowly shrank, except for a few notable exceptions — blue whales, which, at one hundred tons, are the largest mammals that have ever lived, and the eastern coyote, an animal increasing in size right now, just as we are.

Though wolf genes are partly responsible for building up the coyote's size, so is the process of "species divergence," a phrase Darwin coined in *Natural Selection* to describe the way similar species avoided direct competition with each other by fitting themselves into slightly different niches. Where wolves and coyotes had to coexist, they evolved to eat different foods and inhabit different terrain. Where coyotes no longer have to keep out of their bigger cousins' way, they can swell into the best available places for serious eating and growing and sleeping unmolested.

There's an additional reason for coyote growth that's completely interwoven with our own, and it derives quite simply from our abundance, our good food and rich landscapes, our sculpted suburbs that afford so many easy places to hide. As a result, not only are its legs longer and its skull larger than those of coyotes anywhere else, the eastern coyote is also considerably heavier than its relatives in the West. Most of those in the Northeast weigh between 30 and 45 pounds (males), or between 22 and 36 pounds (females), though individual animals have been found well in excess of 50 pounds. That's almost twice as large as the western coyote, making it surely twice as daunting when met face to face on a wooded, narrow trail.

7

WILD TURKEYS TEETER in the trees above the highway, feeding above the ice crust on the berries of bittersweet. Each of the last three snowstorms has been followed by a day of rain and then a freeze. For coyotes this ice sheet means relatively easy travel; their paws act like snowshoes by distributing their body weight, so their journeys over frozen surfaces are faster than for those with hoofed feet. But the deer suffer terribly. If they haven't gathered in herds and formed yards, packing down communal resting places, then they're liable to break through the crust at unpredictable intervals, putting them at risk of broken bones, hypothermia, or starvation, of becoming easy prey for roaming dogs or coyotes.

A heavy kill this winter could renew the request for a coyote bounty, like the penny a pelt for wolves established in 1630. Except it would be in today's dollars, offering an incentive greater than the current market price, which has fluctuated in recent years from $17 to $40 per pelt. It's something I've overheard several times, especially as fewer hunters take to the woods each year. "Put a bigger price on that fur and you'll see them brought in."

But then, I also recently learned of a bounty scam years ago in upstate New York, where money was paid for coyote tails, the experts sure each tail proved there was a dead animal somewhere. As it turned out, however, breeders were raising coyotes and chopping off their tails for cash, while the animals, who survived the process, continued to produce more litters and more profitable tails each spring.

Brutal tactics aside, it's an apt image for the cumulative effect of coyote bounties: they boost populations. Every state that enacted a bounty at some point in its past now has a larger number of resilient coyotes than ever before. Kansas maintained a coyote bounty for some ninety-three years before officials finally concluded that the system had completely failed at reducing their numbers. In Michigan, which paid almost $1.9 million in bounties over the course of thirty-five years, almost the same number of coyotes were killed in 1935 as in 1970, and now the state is at saturation level. In Nova Scotia, wildlife managers were fairly quick to admit that the $50 offered per coyote scalp between 1982 and 1986 had done nothing to slow the arrival of the animal.

In fact, to date it appears that almost every effort to exterminate coyotes has caused the opposite to happen: their numbers have blossomed. Though it's a biological principle true of most species — that when a distinct pressure is applied against it, a corresponding will to survive emerges — seldom is it seen to influence a growth rate this large. The coyote's rate of success has been unparalleled among animals (though rats or gulls must come in a close second). The more money and time spent on eradicating coyotes — increasing the number of traps and snares and detonating devices, or the number of derbies and smoke-outs and aerial shootings — the more adaptable they become.

The one deterrent that has effectively slowed them is Compound 1080, or sodium monofluoroacetate, though the effects of that toxin were so deadly to other creatures that its use was finally halted through a Presidential Executive Order in 1972. Charles Cadieux, who worked for over a decade as a coyote control officer for the U.S. Fish and Wildlife Service, describes its use in *Coyotes: Predators and Survivors*. Firmly believing that "the coyote has been responsible for driving about one half of America's sheep ranchers out of business," Cadieux advocates various methods of control, though each has its limitations.

Direct methods, such as digging out dens and killing the pups or simply tossing smoke cylinders into the burrow and then seal-ing the entrance, involved far too many man-hours for the small number of coyotes killed. Trapping worked up to a point, but "when trapping is intensified, there is some form of communication between coyotes," Cadieux writes; somehow they let each other know whenever steel traps are set in the area. Considerably more effective were the M-44s. A spike is driven into the ground with a bit of bait on top, concealing the small explosive charge set just underneath. When a coyote pulls at the bait, it triggers the charge, which sends cyanide directly into the coyote's mouth. Death happens fast. Unfortunately, M-44s are also effective with foxes and curious dogs.

That left Compound 1080 as the best weapon in the coyote hunter's arsenal. The substance is odorless, tasteless, and extremely effective, according to Cadieux. Nothing about it provides the coyote any warning of its presence, and it causes coyotes to travel after ingesting it, making it less likely that the survivors would connect the death with an obvious cause. A 1080 death, however, "is not pretty," writes Cadieux. "It works on the nervous system so that the vital processes are speeded up — as if the motor had lost its governor and, unregulated, ran itself to destruction . . . Unlike strychnine, which causes a very few sharp convulsions and then quick death, 1080 dooms the animal to several hours of agony before it finally dies." A few bites from a treated carcass and the coyote becomes "extremely nervous and excitable" and runs off at high speed, often dying up to half a mile away.

Preparing the bait was not pretty, either. A live sheep was injected with a solution of 1080 delivered under pressure. "When a bit of pink began to show in the lips of the sheep, the injection was stopped and the sheep killed. Often, the sheep dropped before time to kill it — perhaps a victim of a stroke caused by the added fluid under pressure."

His descriptions both repel and intrigue me, and I find myself wondering again about this desire to kill. In Cadieux's stories it shows up again in his descriptions of hunting coyotes with a rifle; particularly provocative is the pleasure he feels when he's mistaken for *prey*, those brief, lusty moments when it seems a coyote is pursuing him. It happens each time Cadieux uses a coyote caller (a small instrument that a hunter blows or cranks), which sounds like the cry of a dying animal and inevitably brings out any coyotes in the area. "The look in those lemon-yellow eyes . . . is amazing." The coyote rushes guilelessly toward the hunter, thinking *rabbit*, thinking *mouse*. "There is something very exciting about being the hunted, about completely fooling a clever animal . . . [It's] one of the most exciting of all rifle hunting sports." Until the trigger is pulled and the game ends.

The sheer volume of deaths Cadieux tallies in his book makes that pleasure in the kill even more obvious. Between the years 1937 and 1981, the U.S. Fish and Wildlife Service received 3,612,220 coyote scalps, or about 80,000 per year. Cadieux thinks that's only about half of the total killed, however, and that a more realistic number is closer to six million in that forty-five-year span. In a recent article in *Audubon*, Mike Finkel provides more recent statistics, including who's killing the coyotes and what methods they're using. In 1996, Wildlife Service agents killed a total of 82,261 coyotes, including 28,000 shot from the air, 22,000 poisoned by M-44s, 8,000 trapped, and 1,600 killed in their dens. That was but a fraction of the total coyote kills for the year, however. Most of the animals were shot during contests — the Coyote Derby in Montana, the Predator Hunt Spectacular in Arizona, the San Juan Coyote Hunt in New Mexico, the Pennsylvania Coyote Hunt — for a total of 400,000 destroyed in one year. That's more than 1,000 coyotes killed each day, or almost one coyote per minute.

And still, their numbers keep growing.

IN THE CELLAR, I dodge spider webs and the wet spot forming under a slow-dripping faucet. For the first time I see a new leak, probably coming in through the foundation from the melting-warm day. But that's not why I'm here. Something is thumping, and I've already ruled out the refrigerator, the plumbing, and the rocking chair on the floor above, where someone from Holly's poetry group is beating a steady rhythm.

I thought the mouse invasion had slowed. Most mornings now, when I check the traps, they're empty, though I still hear the occasional ceiling scurry; I still wake to find signs of nightly raids — a trail of scat across the silverware and bits of chewed pastry brush scattered about the drawer.

Then I see it: a white-footed mouse, thump-dragging across the floor, one of its rear legs pinned in a trap.

God, I hate these choices. Let it go or kill it fast, the way I once watched a farmer dispatch a deformed chick. A quick twist of its neck, and that was it, the bird spared the agony of death due to starvation, its legs unable to hoist it toward food. Careful to make no sound that might carry into the room where the group is meeting, I hurry back upstairs, return with a pot of water, and drop the mouse in. I hold the trap down with a stick and try to look away, but I can't. It scrabbles at the sides way too long, a sound so desperate, I'm sure the poets must hear it.

But the rise and fall of voices continues and at last the mouse stops moving. It seems to have shrunk to half its former size, the emptying of its life making it seem smaller still.

Outside, I toss it over the fence by the barn, the night bitterly cold, stars sparking in the rimey air. I hope a coyote finds it before it freezes clear through.

Back inside, I scour the pot in water hot enough to scald my hand. And then I wonder, as the hurt slows me down, whether the next time I cook pasta or steam vegetables I'll taste fear, the saliva of an animal sucking for air and getting water, the urine squirt that occurs when organs are forced to quit.

I scrub absurdly long.

. . .

I DROWNED AN ANIMAL once before, when I lived on Deer Isle in Maine. I wanted to be cavalier about it, like the people who dispatch puppies when there's no money to feed them and no takers to give them new homes; like the ones who lower the sack of kittens into the creek because the area is already saturated with housecats, barn cats, and abandoned cats turned wild.

But I wasn't able to muster nonchalance.

I drowned it because I had trapped it, and because I wanted to take responsibility for what I did in the world, even if my world was only the size of an island. I drowned it because I was tired of the trade in small mammals in which I'd been an unwitting participant.

For a while it had made sense, when I caught raccoons in the Havahart trap, to take them over the bridge and let them go on the mainland. That was what the whole "have-a-heart" concept was about, a trap-and-release program that let us feel benevolent and resourceful. For a raccoon, the other side of the bridge offered far better land, most of it forested and far less peopled than the island. But then stories started surfacing of people on the mainland doing the same thing, in the reverse order — catching skunks and raccoons and porcupines in live traps, driving them to the island, and letting them go where they were easily contained in a small and finite place.

The mainland farmer nearest the bridge finally strung Christmas lights around his corn in an attempt to keep raccoons from harvesting more than their share. On the island, the garbage fights grew fiercer. Loose-lidded trash cans made for the easiest raids, along with pet food dishes, bird feeders, and barrels used to store seed. The raccoon that plagued me got all the ripe strawberries and sliced screens on the porch. Then he opened the door and let himself in, helping himself to handfuls of leftovers and leaving greasy wet prints.

Our Quaker discussion group took on the topic of problem

animals. I was surprised to hear the elders advocate shooting them — the porcupines destroying fruit trees, the raccoons sampling the best of the harvest. No one mentioned deer, however, a protected species eating its own food supply faster than it could be replenished, as though there were no correlation between aiming a gun at a slowly moving, quill-covered, tiny-brained porcupine, and pointing that same weapon at a large-boned, sensitive-faced, poetry-in-motion deer.

Quakers, who find "that of the Light" in everyone (and, for some, in every living thing), were finding consensus in dispatch. Practical men and women, wise and thoughtful and conscientious, unanimous in their approach to the issue. For them, it wasn't a dilemma; the solution was simple.

I smeared peanut butter on the bait tray and caught the fat raccoon. And then I had to contemplate my options.

I could've taken it to the ocean and waded out to my knees, but I didn't want to be seen.

I could've put the trap in a large plastic bag, rigged a hose from the car's exhaust, and ended the animal's life with carbon monoxide.

Instead, I put the garden hose in an empty barrel and filled it with water. Then I dropped the trap in.

It wasn't simple. The raccoon leveraged its way to the top, its hands reaching through the cage to grab the barrel's edge. I got a stick and pushed down. The raccoon pushed up, its white-rimmed eyes as clear to me now as they were then. But my fear at that point was as big. I pushed down harder and won, and in a mixture of revulsion and rage vowed I would never set a live trap again.

FIFTEEN YEARS LATER, in an evening class at the college, I hear a collective voice from the students that would have condemned me on the spot if they knew what I had done. We had reached the point in the semester where we shift from analyzing the content of an essay to looking at the techniques an author uses to convey those main points. George Orwell's "Shooting an Elephant" seemed a useful example of several narrative techniques, as Orwell recounted experiences as a police officer in British-controlled India. We're only a few minutes into the period, however, when a response spills out that I wasn't expecting, an anger that allows no distance, no perspective on the reading.

They can't appreciate Orwell's style because they have been trained to resist any details that might involve killing — of an animal, that is. These are not students of postcolonial theory; they have no sense of a British empire in India, or of the resistant population the English sought to control. They know, quite simply, that Orwell, who is called to respond when an elephant escapes and kills a man in the process, has given horrific details of the way he dispatches the huge animal. Reading it was like "witnessing a torture," says one student. "I couldn't finish it," says another. "I couldn't understand why he had to shoot an innocent creature."

"It was disgusting," says a third, and I find us far away from the assignment's main points, certain derailment if I can't get us back on track.

Maybe if I had slept better last night, if unrest weren't seeping steadily through our house, then I wouldn't feel so keenly the students' silence about that other death — of the coolie the elephant caught by surprise and ground into the earth. "The friction of the great beast's foot had stripped the skin from his back as neatly as one skins a rabbit," writes Orwell. "His face was coated with mud, the eyes wide open, the teeth bared and grinning with an expression of unendurable agony."

It's the death of the elephant that stirs the students' rage.

Eventually, a quiet woman who is finding her place as a moderating presence in the class addresses Orwell's expressed conflict about his role. She suggests that the coolie's death captures much of the way the local people were treated by the British, the elephant a metaphor for Britain's role in the East. But the younger students reign tonight, and they're on a roll about abuses done to animals. *(Chemicals sprayed in the eyes of laboratory rabbits! Cancers grown in their bodies! Pain inflicted merely to see what they can and cannot stand!)* And though I want to agree with them — cruelty should be avoided no matter who or what the target — tonight I can't see the world through their eyes. I feel old and far away from such limited, righteous passion.

I distribute a handout describing the next assignment, and while they read it over, I consider the way the animal rights movement has established pain as the moral center of the universe. The big decisions these students will make, or so their arguments suggest, will be based primarily on the presence or absence of pain. Of course, this might not be too different from having God or love or justice at life's core, but the strength of their feelings and the seeming inconsistency of their criteria (their tattoos and multiple piercings intimate a certain callousness about pain) suggest the pendulum will swing again before we arrive in a more balanced place when considering our relationship with animals. As it stands right now, at least in what I heard tonight, the relationship seems raw and unseasoned. A man was killed by the elephant, and only one student remarked on it, as though animals rate a higher place than humans and we who would protect them matter less because of this obligation. And though on the one hand I'm glad to hear students take responsibility for righting the wrongs done to those less powerful, on the other hand it highlights our differing definitions of "responsibility."

While they might circulate one of the brochures used in the campaign to pass the Wildlife Protection Act in Massachusetts, a photo of a terrified housecat caught in a leghold trap on its cover, I might counter with questions on the implications of the measure. As a humane concept, the idea of banning all leghold traps is ap-

pealing, yet it also means far fewer ways of responding when predators become too comfortable with the slovenly ways of humans.
What would these students suggest doing if the glossy image were
of a coyote holding the cat in its mouth? What if ten coyotes lived
under the garage? What if a rabid coyote were coming up the
walk, swinging its head and frothing at the mouth? What would
they see as an appropriate response then?

And who should take responsibility for the edges where we
and coyotes meet?

That's when I get it. I'm as defensive as they are, and for similar reasons. They want to regulate behavior on their own terms,
much as I did at their age and often still do. They're poised to
speak out against the killing of any animal. They want to dictate
what happens at circuses and fashion shows, at sportsmen's hunts
and cosmetics labs. And while I, too, want to control what happens in the world immediately around me, I also want these students to see the larger balancing act we all have to do in a world
where predators pursue prey, killing happens regularly, and these
deaths are never determined by degrees of pain or moral codes. In
the woods and fields outside the windows of this school, most mo-
ment-to-moment decisions have to do with food and shelter and
the protection of a gene pool, not the possibility or avoidance of
pain.

But that's the subject of another class, another setting, and
I'm still not ready to admit the degree to which pain has become
an occupying force in my own home.

8

My youngest brother calls; he has exhausted child-care options and do I have any days free during his daughter's school vacation? Immediately, it's easy to put aside homework and make plans to spend time with an eight-year-old girl.

We pick out presents for Holly's upcoming birthday and devise ways to keep them secret; we eat at a fast-food restaurant and play all the words games on the packaging; then we decide to risk the glaze of ice that covers the ground and we head for the field behind my childhood home, where lately my parents have seen a saw-whet owl.

The day is overcast and still, the smell of spring hovers under the trees, and there's just enough melt to make walking feel possible. We find the hemlock where the owl has been spotted; we scan the nearby trees; we try to imagine what an owl wants for a perch and a view. And when we don't see it anywhere, we realize we'd rather walk to the river.

Its sounds can be heard well before we see it, a churning-fast, enticing rush, and then it's below us, green and full and dark. We take the path to Red Rock, a sandstone ledge with a swimming hole just below it, then start wandering upstream. For Chloe that means rushing again and again to the river's edge — where a small stream tumbles down and forms long icicles above the deeper water, where the line of horsetails thins and forms a natural opening, where a thick rope sways from a high branch, and where we stop and look down with dismay. Anyone who grabbed hold, swung out, and dropped would land on a ledge rather than in a pool. Bruised, we agree, rather than cooled.

A well-packed animal path takes us alongside the river, but we can't decide if it was made by a mink or an otter. Or a raccoon, up and down the bank, looking for places to gather mussels.

So many times I almost say, "This is where I used to . . ." and each time I catch myself, letting it be as new for her as it was for me at her age.

She fishes cool rocks from an icy brook, not seeming to mind the chill against her bare fingers. Fallen logs become bridges, icy slopes another test of her balance. She is long-legged like her parents and comfortable in her tall body. Meanwhile, I fall hard once, the bang of my head like a single basketball bounce. When I confirm I'm not hurt, we laugh at the words "hard-headed" and "numbskull," and while I wait for the ringing in my ears to stop, we watch two black ducks watch us, until something sends them hurrying into flight.

After that, Chloe is quick to warn me about more icy patches, while pointing out new sights — the perfect circle of ice around a stick dangling in the river, the dark bands around each horsetail stem, the glint of mica in a stream-washed rock, the layer of colors in the clay bank, in the ice, in the red sandstone underneath.

I delay turning back until we have just enough time to make our rendezvous with her dad, not wanting to lose this feeling that a familiar place can seem untraveled, each object called into being when touched by a curious girl.

WALKING THE WOODS ALONE is not as much fun as with Chloe, nor do I walk in that same rushing, sudden way. I travel slowly. My senses hover; every cell feels ready. Give me a spoor, a hair, a cracking stick, and I'll immediately puzzle out the options — what it is and where and how many.

With coyotes, however, how many might be impossible to tell. They might pass by in a group of four or five, family members hunting together through the winter, but the track, particularly if

there's much snow, might announce the presence of just one animal. The trick — called "direct registering" — is actually the imprint of one foot atop another, one animal's track fitting inside the
print of the animal in front of it, a brilliant technique for disguis-
ing numbers.

It's simple and fluid and remarkable, a group of animals moving as one synchronized unit. And it's something domestic dogs
can't do, nor have they any need to try. For them, concealment
isn't necessary. At a walk, a dog leaves sloppy, overlapped pairs.
But the walking gait of a coyote is quite precise, its hind foot falling in the very spot where its forepaw had been, an exact match of
back and front toes, a neat fit of fore and rear heel pads. The coyote traveling behind the first animal lands in the same spot; the
coyote behind does the same, creating a rhythmic, consistently accurate track. It's a trait of all the canids — coyotes, foxes, wolves
— and is a key feature in identifying their trails: straight, narrow
lines of prints, single file patterns of directly registered tracks.
(Wild cats can do it, too, but they leave no claw marks.)

I want to see them do it. I want to find pad prints and know
speeds and numbers now, in this dusting of new snow that sticks to
the ice just enough to afford a small measure of traction.

But it's impossible to walk quietly on this surface. My footsteps boom; I sound violent and ungainly. I'm not as loud, however, as the all-terrain vehicle that churns through the white pines
toward me, nor am I as fast. Instead of ducking off the trail and
trying to hide (not possible in my down parka, which doubles my
width), I wait for the approach. It's a good decision: two large
German shepherds race ahead of their owner, and they surely
would have nosed me out. When the driver gets within a few feet,
he quiets the throttle and pulls off his helmet. "Out for a nature
walk?" he asks.

I nod.

"I'm just running the dogs," he says. "Giving them some exercise." He watches them bound away and then looks back at me, sheepish and shrugging. "You scared me, you know. I never see anyone out here."

I live nearby, I tell him, I come out when I can. Then we both look away. Eventually I express my surprise that his big machine doesn't break through the crust. "The ice is too thick," he says and pats a fender. "In conditions like this, it's the only way to travel."

After he leaves, I follow his trail but see nothing other than the tracks of his dogs and one set of grouse prints in a dense sumac stand. I still hear his "nature walk" comment, however, and I think about another child I recently spent time with, a girl whose mother has been friends with Holly since high school. When they visited us in Tallahassee, Christa and I headed for the woods, where she was as interested as Chloe in butterflies, damselflies, birds' nests, and animal holes. When we reached the brook, she yanked off her shoes and waded into a concentrated world of wildlife — spiders overhead, water striders on the surface, a snowy egret startled into flight. We urged crawfish out of crevices and minnows out of hiding and climbed onto the bank only after she pointed out a small snake. "Look," she said, "a water moccasin."

Later, when we returned with feathers and shells and balls of clay, she told everyone who would listen, "There's so much nature here!"

Her words overlap in my mind with those of the man on the ATV, and I hear each of them naming Nature as though it were a containable thing, a world with finite edges and somehow separate from us. The concept feels odd, like pulling some great screen up and down. The screen's up, we're in nature; it's down and we're not.

Yet what I think they mean is the difference between outside and in, which for me has more to do with what I can and can't control. Inside I can exert some influence over heat, food, mice; a place that's dry when it rains, warm when it's cold, sheltered when the winds blow hard. Outside, though I carve out gardens, a lawn, flowerbeds, paths, I can't truly affect the result because there are rabbits and deer and moles and cabbage moths and droughts and days of too much acid rain. And because I can't control it, I surrender to its workings, another heart with a beat, another strand in the web.

When I leave the chained-tire marks and head home, I practice walking in my earlier footsteps. It takes all my concentration to fit each foot into the exact shape of the previous print.

9

IN THE PAST few weeks, three different people, regular observers of the world outside their windows, have told me about the huge wolf they've just seen. "But wolves don't exist here anymore," I say. I state it quietly, because I know that these animals are appearing at dusk under the bird feeder, or at the edge of the lawn, or near the open door of the garage, their shapes so unexpected and large that of course the first association is *wolf*. "It was probably a coyote," I say, and see each person's sudden distrust of me, their certainty that I don't know what I'm talking about.

But I understand how fear inflates shapes. My older brother used to look bigger; so have strangers I'm not sure of. Fear can turn vines into snakes, stumps into alligators, shadows into bodies with malicious intent. Yet desire exerts an equally strong force, altering what we see into what we want — a tic into a smile, a cow into a deer, a series of numbers into the sequence that won a lottery. Then the moment shifts, someone supplies binoculars, or a store clerk reads the winning numbers aloud.

Such visual tricks are so common that names have been coined to describe them — "premature closure" or "early blur," for those moments when we catch an outline or shadow of a thing we think we recognize and automatically fill in the missing pieces. Either phenomenon might facilitate the transformation of coyotes into wolves, at least for those of us east of the Mississippi, where wolves are the only large canids that dwell in our psychic spaces. The briefest reminder — a howl in a movie's soundtrack, a loping animal in a rearview mirror — and we supply the associations: This scene's going to become even more dangerous.

For most of us, coyote images don't immediately surface in our brains; we have no ingrained response to their sudden size and shape. We have a few negative associations with an animal they resemble in coloring — the German shepherd — but that's for a specific behavior, the snarling, teeth-bared, police dog's fury. We don't have fixed images for the more benign coyote behaviors — an animal leaping high in a field after mice, lapping up bird seed under a feeder, or loping in midday across a college campus. If we catch the sight for but a second, when passing in a car or by a window, most of us wouldn't say, *A coyote, feeding.* Surprise and proximity would compel us to say, *Wolf.*

Yet a coyote sighting is increasingly likely for anyone living in the East — if that first encounter hasn't already happened. Each of my coyote firsts, from the years I lived in Vermont, is a clean and clear memory, untainted by anything I knew or wanted then. And it happened slowly enough — the first coyote that strolled past my house, the coyote I watched fade into a field, the coyotes tilting back their heads in a wild nighttime chorus.

Final sightings are far harder to mark. Few people knew it was all over for the Carolina parakeet, the passenger pigeon, the heath hen. Few stood in their doorways as the last birds were felled by hunters and understood that their grandchildren would never see such sights again. The numbers, after all, had once been greater than the thousands of ladybugs that have hatched this spring.

I listen to them click and knock against the windows, watch them circle walls that are warming in the sun, and can't imagine our world will ever be without them. A quick estimate yields 200 that I can see at this moment. Multiplied by the 800 or so houses in this village, multiplied again by the 250 or so other small towns in the state — excluding the cities too big for me to calculate — is something like 40 million ladybugs in Massachusetts alone, and that's counting just the ones that winter in buildings; another kind of ladybug gathers by the thousands in leaf litter and hollow trees, in safe, dark places alongside hidden streams.

And yet experience tells me that ladybugs, too, could die off, the way the heath hen did, the way the Eskimo curlew might do next, if, in fact, any still exist. I would have liked to see either one — the heath hen for its distinct wail during mating season, which some called cacophonous, others "ghostly and otherworldly," and the curlew for its soft whistle and its ability to fly some 8,000 miles, a chunky small bird migrating from high in western Canada to the southernmost regions of Argentina.

The heath hen, with its triumphant lover's name, *Tympanuchus cupido cupido*, and brilliant orange sacks that flared on the males' necks during mating, was easier to hit than a tin duck at a shooting gallery. By 1835, they had been hunted off the mainland, with but a small colony persisting on Martha's Vineyard for another hundred years. For the Eskimo curlew, a similar fate is in the offing, if it isn't already extinct. Estimates vary from fifty to one hundred birds still alive somewhere in the wild, but that number is a guess at best. Its recovery seems slim, though its numbers were once so huge that flocks of the "doughbirds," fattened for their long journey south, once clouded the sky as though storms were coming. For a few excessive decades in the mid-1800s, all those clouds were emptied, the birds shipped in trainloads to the cities filled with insatiable hungers.

My grandmother may have seen one of the last of these curlews in 1976 on the north shore of Massachusetts. She caught the color, the size, the thin, decurved bill; she knew it was a rarity, but she didn't yet know how scarce. Two other people saw what must have been the same bird later that afternoon. They, too, knew it to be an Eskimo curlew, though the three wouldn't compare notes until several days later.

None of them knew they might have been seeing a last living

specimen, that someone should have organized a farewell party, quickly, with dignitaries and photographers and maybe some cake. Yet surely we would be as negligent, if but one or two ladybugs were to show up next year, as unaware that we should hurry with our thanks, commissioning portraits and videos before the last beetle flew off.

Chances are far greater, however, that ladybugs will follow this new coyote model, a lesson in abundance that helps dispel such bleak thinking. With the current explosion in ladybug numbers — supplemented by the importation of millions from Asia — anyone can now have the insects gracing their home.

Similarly, anyone living anywhere in this country now has a good chance of seeing their first coyote, of forming that initial impression. Of course, the movement of the animal — whether it arches or lopes, startles or skulks — will do as much as early blur in determining how it is perceived, and how it is remembered.

As I PULL a meatloaf from the oven for tonight's community meal, I wonder how many people will show up, whether someone will bring bread or dessert, whether there will be enough hot food, enough milk; whether we'll see lots of small children and no empty seats or thirty adults in a half-full room and plenty of leftovers to divvy up afterward.

It's a ritual I've grown to like, along with the fact that it's time spent with my mother, our serving group one she's helped organize for over fifteen years. It's something to work at, side by side, having nothing to do with family or grandkids, with ways we're alike and ways we're different, and everything to do with sharing what we have with others who have less. And each Tuesday that we do this, I learn more about this community, the people I saw as a child, the people who arrived after I left. It's another way to gauge the changes that have taken place in the last two decades, another way to see the expectations I bring to those around me.

I wasn't here for the David-and-Goliath struggle the town

won against Wal-Mart, keeping the retail giant out and the small downtown area alive and vital. I wasn't around for the seizure of a local couple's house, which the IRS auctioned, amid occupations by protesters, to collect the taxes the antiwar activists had long refused to pay. And I hadn't yet arrived when the news finally broke about a family that had tortured and murdered a retarded man in their care, without anyone — neighbors, relatives, social workers — trying to intervene.

Participants in any of those events might be here tonight; there's no way for me to tell, as I spoon food onto plates and catch up on other ongoing stories, about the man teaching himself to design Web pages, about the woman who feels brave enough at last to sing in a community chorus, about the grandson who has finally mastered math. People respond to this abundance in various ways. Some heap their plates, others carefully pick and choose; some dump what they don't like, get refills, and start over, while others stay in their seats until everything is eaten; some rush for dessert, filling bags and pockets with cookies, others tentatively ask if it's all right to have seconds.

As I serve and eat, jostle and help clean up, I make sure to notice not only the comfortable sameness but the less obvious changes as well — the man who might be getting back on his feet, the woman who might be slipping away from us. It's a forced way of seeing that I always keep brief.

IN THE CLEARING at the top of the field, I tilt my face back and feel March, a warmth I haven't known since October. Sumac branches appear lit, the sun animating their hairy softness. Chickadees and kinglets chatter as they work along twigs, ceaselessly hunting for the soft bodies of insects and larvae, while a breeze rattles the stiff vines of bittersweet and grape. Otherwise it's still — at least on the surface. For somewhere, within a few square miles of here, a pair of coyotes is cleaning out a den, most likely an

old woodchuck burrow that they're making a little larger, the female swelling with the young taking shape inside her.

In this odd, icy winter, they may have mated anywhere from late January to early March, with the female ready to whelp nine weeks later, sixty-three days from fertilization to birth. The moment of intercourse is critical — that sheltered pause the coyotes found between ice storms and flattening winds, between the intrusions of hunters, whose season on coyotes coincides with their mating, and the rush of dogs that escape leashes and race through these woods. The dogs would find coyotes in the act of mating quite easy to brutalize, the locked-together position leaving them vulnerable to assault. It's the success of that moment of fertilization that determines if and when pups will arrive, mid-March at the very earliest, more likely the first week of April.

Soon I shall know how the coyote who scavenged dead mice near the barn and the one who left its mark on the trail fared this winter. Soon I hope to find where they den and learn who inherits the role of helper, the unmated young adult who stays near the new family, warning the smallest pups of danger or assisting in feeding the fast-growing litter. This spring I want to be fast enough to see them before they melt into underbrush and quiet enough to hear the press of steps as they disappear.

A ruffed grouse, unable to stay silent any longer, explodes out of the snow about ten feet from where I'm standing and beats hard for deeper woods.

When I regain my calm, I too move on, surprised by all I fail to see, even when I think I'm paying attention. And then, in the field at the top of the next hill, I find pussywillows, small and tight and welcome.

10

MORNINGS BEGIN NOW with a rush of sound, a frenzy of finches, robins, cardinals, titmice. In the valley the whistles of song sparrows spiral around the cries of redwings and killdeer. Daffodil bulbs knuckle up in the lawn. Buds of lilac and forsythia bulge from their stems. A band of red from birches and maples widens in the hills, and I want to make lists, capturing the speed of all the changes, naming all that arrives with each new minute of light.

Mostly I want to move the season even faster so I can till the garden and start transplanting seedlings. But the last frost might not occur until the end of May, and other than setting out sturdy young broccoli plants and sowing some cold-hardy seeds like peas and beets, it's schoolwork I have to concentrate on, a good distraction from the buildup of pain in the house. The sight of Holly's cheeks, which swell with the hurt of a deteriorating hip joint, makes clear that I need to stay within calling range.

I temper my impatience by hunting for coyotes inside, beginning with Holly's one-volume *Oxford English Dictionary*. With a magnifying glass to help read the tiny print, I find that coyote comes from *coyotl*, a Mexican word for the barking wolf of the Pacific slope of North America. Other early spellings include "cayeute," "cayote," "cayjotte," and "cocyotie." From a work published in 1824: "Mexico produces an animal which seems to connect the wolf, fox, and dog; it is called the cocyotie." By 1846 another writer was referring to "the cayeute . . . or medicine-wolf of the Indians," and by 1849 the author of *California* noted that "a

75

species of jackal, called here the coyote, frequently approached within a few rods of us." At first glance it appears that this etymological journey offers more evidence of the animal's slow expansion northward. But the safer conclusion is that the apparent trajectory from Mexico to California and then north and east is not so much the coyote's as it is the timeline of arrivals for those first describing coyote encounters in English.

Mark Twain was one of them. He devotes a short chapter to coyotes in *Roughing It*, that tongue-in-cheek account of his brief stint in the Wild West, after he realized that being a Confederate soldier was more dangerous to the Confederacy than it was to himself and lit out for the territories with his Unionist brother, Orion. Of the coyote, Twain writes that it is "a long, slim, sick and sorry-looking skeleton, with a gray wolfskin stretched over it. He is *always* hungry. He is always poor, out of luck, and friendless . . . He is so spiritless and cowardly that even while his exposed teeth are pretending a threat, the rest of his face is apologizing for it. And he is *so* homely! — so scrawny, and ribby, and coarse-haired, and pitiful." Yet that pitiful creature also takes great delight in outwitting any dog that might pursue it, at which point the shamefaced dog "turns and jogs along back to the train, and takes up a humble position under the hindmost wagon, and feels unspeakably mean, and looks ashamed, and hangs his tail at half-mast for a week."

Twain ends the section with a biting comparison of Indians to coyotes, "kin" that eat the same dead things, both surviving in the most desolate waste places of the world, hating all other creatures "and yearning to assist at their funerals." Even in the context of his impatience with those who romanticized "The Noble Red Man," the insult is extreme.

Another writer of the same period, whose notes about Indians appeared posthumously in *The Maine Woods*, also had a blind spot to the Native American experience, at least according to

Charles Leland, who takes Thoreau to task for his complete lack of understanding of the oral tradition of his native guides. Thoreau deliberately sought out Penobscot Indians who could lead him up Maine rivers and reveal to him some of their secrets, yet according to Leland, he was dismissive of their storytelling abilities. "An Indian," writes Thoreau, "tells such a story as if he thought it deserved to have a good deal said about it, only he has not got it to say; and so he makes up for the deficiency by a drawling tone, long-windedness and a dumb wonder which he hopes will be contagious."

Leland, a folklorist who spent the last decades of the nineteenth century collecting stories from the eastern Woodland tribes, mocks the remark as "singularly characteristic of Mr. Thoreau's own nasal stories about Nature." Had Thoreau understood Indian legends, Leland observes, he might have spoken more wisely of their poetry and their myths. Instead, "such a writer can, indeed, peep and botanize on the grave of Mother Nature, but can never evoke *her* spirit."

To provide a context for understanding the narrative traditions of Native Americans, Leland gathered hundreds of their stories for his collection *Algonquin Legends*. It's a resource I look to for proof that coyotes had no past here, that they weren't what early colonialists identified as brush wolves. In tale after tale, I find no evidence of coyotes, no descriptions like those in the stories of western tribes where coyotes are seen as comic or pathetic, eating offal and old leather and scraps grabbed from boiling soup pots.

In western stories, coyotes pass as sheep or old women, trusted friends or shifty children, maybe even buffalo if they can keep their small feet hidden. Or they die and then race through the house, or are dismembered and then appear at the dinner table, ready to share in the meal that's about to be served. And that ratty hide that Twain mentioned? It appears often in stories from the other side of the Mississippi and is explained in this way by Simon Ortiz: Coyote once had a gorgeous coat, but he gambled it away. Fortunately, the mice who saw him shivering felt so sorry for him that they helped repair the loss by gluing scraps of fur to his naked body, using piñon pitch to make them stick.

Nothing comes close to this character in tales from the eastern tribes — those comprising the Algonquin, Abnaki, or Iroquois federations. There is no coyote prankster. There is, however, a remarkable spirit-man who embodies many of the same traits of the western coyote, though in most accounts he is also far more powerful. Called Glooskap by the Micmac and Gluscabi by the Penobscot, this hero was a force of good who often interceded between naive humans and the Great Spirit. His was the first birth in the world, according to Wabanaki legend, and he was the one who created humans from the ash tree. He also named the birds and animals and presented humans with fire.

Yet he's usually portrayed with as much humor as reverence. According to Joseph Bruchac, a contemporary Abnaki poet and storyteller, even though Glooskap had great powers, he "sometimes made mistakes." These "mistakes," as Leland relates them, were typically the result of blunders or the consequence of Glooskap's irresistible impulse to play jokes on unsuspecting humans.

The wolf is the big canid that sometimes appears in eastern tales, and he's usually cast in marked contrast to Glooskap's role of good-humored trickster. In a Wabanaki creation tale, he is Glooskap's twin brother, Malsum, a wolf who embodies evil much as Glooskap manifests good. The two roam the earth, attempting, at times, to kill or sabotage the other, with Glooskap usually prevailing. In other versions of this story, however, there is no wolf, no malevolent presence; instead, Glooskap travels the world with a dog who functions as helper and companion.

The eastern tribes had another character who bears some physical resemblance to the mischievous coyote — the impish Lox, who may take the form of a wolf, a wolverine, a lynx, or a raccoon, in equal parts ferocious and cunning. "While Glooskap is always a gentleman," writes Leland, "Lox ranges from Punch to Satan." Lox's similarities to the western Coyote include his ability to change sex, to call together his body parts after being dismembered, or to wake up inside a boiling dinner pot, grab his hide off the hook where it was left to dry, and instantly recover his life. As with the western Coyote, Lox's jokes range from tricking old women into attacking each other, to elaborate public embarrassments of local braggarts.

What complicates any research on coyotes in these stories, however, is that there is no clear distinction made between actual wolves and the "wolf-like dogs" that lived with Indians long before Europeans arrived. (That Indians in the Northeast had dogs has long been known, though recent DNA testing suggests that the animals were not native to the New World but derived from Eurasian dogs, presumably brought from Asia thousands of years earlier when a land bridge existed across the Bering Straits.) This makes tracing early canine references particularly challenging, and even in the birchbark drawings that accompany *Algonquin Legends*, Lox looks more like a coyote than a wolverine or lynx. What seems safe to conclude is that the eastern coyote has no immediate ancestry here, no place in the native tradition.

The nonlocal narratives have already had an influence, though, and for the most part they include the most motley and unpleasant of physical traits. Coyotes hunker; they slouch. They're susceptible to the messiest canine diseases — heartworm, distemper, mange. And their particular method of attacking large prey (sheep, calves, young or wounded deer) makes them especially loathsome: they go for the rear end. They pull down calves or yearlings from behind, and once the animal is down, they start feeding then and there, too, going after the guts. They begin at the hind end, "where the skin is thin," explains Paul Rezendes in *Tracking and the Art of Seeing*, "and there is easy access to good portions of meat. They eat until only the head, the legs from the knees down, and the rumen (stomach contents) are left." They'll break ribs while they're at it and haul away shin bones for later gnawing.

And if, when they're hungry, they pass you in their travels, they might fix unblinking yellow eyes on you or your dog, a look that won't let you escape, as in a story I recently heard from Rebekkah Tippens, who lives in Colrain. A coyote parked himself in her backyard one day, which wasn't unusual — "they pass through here all the time" — except that this one overstayed its visit, maintaining an unflinching gaze far too long. That laserlike stare, at her and then at her small collie, produced a sensation that "still pierced her many days later."

This stare — this ability to lock on prey — helps a predator cull out the weak members of a herd, part of the conversation of death that Lopez describes. But I'm curious what it means to have a coyote fix on an adult, and what circumstances could bring such a situation about. I wonder what would happen if, say, I fell and broke a leg while in a remote corner of the Mohawk State Forest. Days can go by without human visitors to the area, when coyotes and bears are the primary inhabitants. I wonder if a coyote would lock on me then, whether fear would be the first emotion to surface, and whether it could possibly transmute into awe.

I didn't catch the gaze from the few I saw before moving here. Instead I saw what was attractive about each animal — strength, agility, power, features that help me resist the lousier images I keep encountering. Such traits make me susceptible to something gladder and more infectious, particularly when recounted by John Foster, a naturalist who spends far more time outside than in.

"Each time I see a coyote," he says, "I'm struck by its beauty, its majesty, and the size of its thighs."

That's where I'd like the story of the eastern coyote to begin.

II

WHEN I FIRST WALKED this land, I had a feeling that all the years and journeys of my adulthood would make sense if I could just live on these few acres and root around in this dirt. I couldn't admit that out loud, however; as potential buyers, we couldn't reveal the size of our desire.

But I had seen enough during those two hours to be seduced — a view of Mt. Massamet, with the stone tower on its summit; the canes of black-capped raspberries so laden that berries fell off as we passed; the large, weed-covered lawn; the back field grown high in saplings; the brook trickling along one edge. When the sellers refused our offer, I took to my bed with a sudden fever and chills. Fortunately, they were in the more awkward position. They had already bought a house elsewhere and were stuck with an empty dwelling that looked seedier with each passing week. We started a second round of negotiations, eventually they lowered their price, and soon the house was ours.

It was never the house that spoke to me, however, with its odd layout and narrow staircase, its chopped-up kitchen and dark living room. I yearned to inhabit the outside.

It's that same yearning that pulls me today. Unable to settle anywhere inside, I wander to a clearing under the pines. I duck to fit under the lower branches, which spread a good forty feet in their reach for the sun, and immediately find quiet inside the sheltered circle, with soft moss underfoot and air pungent with resin. Wild lily-of-the-valley grows around the edge, along with birch saplings and sarsaparilla. Farther down the slope, jewelweed spreads along the brook banks, as do jack-in-the-pulpits that have lost their cowls, exposing stalks of fat seeds. From here I can see what's coming from any direction; I can hear the buzz of insects in the field. But I hadn't expected what's right in front of me — the scat of coyote, recent enough to have been left last night.

I want to shout my joy.

Instead I use a stick to poke it apart, its contents a lot like the inside of a vacuum cleaner bag — compressed hair and fuzz, dust and lint. But farther inside, tucked between dense layers of hair, I find the skeleton of a rodent paw, its tiny bones perfectly jointed; a flattened rib cage, smaller than my smallest fingernail; two cat-claw sheaths; and two jaw bones with rows of miniature molars. This field must provide good hunting — I've seen fat meadow voles run across it, even in the light of day — and I wish coyotes would feed here more often and keep all the rodents at bay.

I'd like to watch them in the act of hunting mice, that sleek

curve of back humping into sight above the tall grass, a sudden pounce to pin the animal. I'd like to see them eat some of these wild blueberries, too, the way I saw a fox do once, or leap across the snow like another fox whose tracks I found one bitter winter morning after the solstice. That fox had leapt again and again in the night, perhaps tossing and playing with a mouse the way a cat will. But in my mind, it had been swept up by the light of the moon in the clear, frigid air and had jumped and spun through the twilight, a dance to music only it could hear, touching down on its hind feet and taking off again and again until at last the urge was spent. Its stomach growled, its partner yipped, and it shook out the last rhythm and resumed its search for food.

It takes a while, pulling weeds, before I realize I'm not the only large presence in the field. I sense the other being before I hear it; I feel its moving body before I catch the snort of air, the toss of its head to get rid of annoying flies. Soon I can hear the workings of its jaw as it bites off branches, the rending sound as it grabs another clump of leaves. I can feel the sinking of sharp hooves in soft earth as it makes its way through thick brush. I know it senses me, too, and so long as I do nothing threatening and don't turn and fix my gaze on it, it will continue to feed, and I will continue to pinch these small weeds. We'll both be warmed by the sun and cooled by the breeze, and life will go on apace.

It's like the situation that a farmer recently described to me, saying that as long as he stays on his tractor, coyotes will feed a short distance away, scarfing up the mice that the mower knocks from their nests. Yet if he turns off the engine or climbs off the seat, the coyotes disappear, nowhere to be seen.

I settle into how companionable this feels, realizing it has been a while since I've felt such familiarity with a wild animal, though there have been several insects of late that I have looked on as neighbors — the spider high in the corner of the bathroom ceiling, the caterpillar that lived on parsley sprigs I kept in a jar on the windowsill, the praying mantis in the tub of iris on the deck. At the time, each seemed a necessary, living part of the day, a being I greeted and looked out for.

Without turning my head, I catch the snap of tail, the deer visible now in a gap between saplings. It watches me as it chews, its ears and tail in steady motion, before leaning down for another bite. It's tempting to mimic it, to begin grazing on tender lettuce, to further this commensal relationship. Instead I enjoy the concept of "commensal," meaning, as an adjective, both eating at the same table and living peacefully with another, and, as a noun, both the meal companion or the companionable animal or plant.

"Commensal" is also the term Ray Coppinger uses in his theory of how dogs were domesticated. According to Coppinger, who has also studied coyotes, domestication wasn't imposed on wild dogs; it was something they did themselves, an idea that radically departs from the long-held belief that humans were the active party in the taming of dogs. As Coppinger sees it, dogs didn't come to people; dogs came to the part of the landscape that was created as soon as groups of humans started living in one place — the village dump. About 15,000 years ago, so his theory goes, about the same time that dogs and wolves differentiated from their common gene pool, wild dogs saw the trash piles as an easy source of food, an ease that helped determine their subsequent shape. Natural selection for dump-feeders produced animals that weren't as quick to bolt — the flight distance for wild dogs was far less than for wolves — nor did they need to be as strong-jawed and sturdy as the wolves, which could easily break the bones of large prey. As the tolerant and increasingly streamlined dogs lingered, people began to realize that their presence was of some assistance to the village — for giving warning signals when danger approached or for helping track certain animals. A commensal relationship was thus begun, of parallel, companionable lives.

It's an appealing theory, based on several compelling points. The first is the belief that dogs and wolves were beginning to differentiate at about the same time that humans were forming permanent settlements (though this notion, too, is hotly contested, with some scientists claiming that the divergence happened at least 135,000 years ago). A second piece of Coppinger's reasoning is the difference in the respective flight distances required by the two species. For the wolf, this distance is considerable; it can't tolerate having a human approach beyond a certain threshold, at which point the wolf flees. The newly evolving dog, however, must have been genetically tamer and able to tolerate a much closer approach; it continued to forage long after the wolf was gone, thereby aiding its specialization for the refuse niche. A third point is that dogs, according to Coppinger, just aren't very smart; they don't have the wolf's brain or the coyote's adaptability, and as a consequence (my logical extension of his argument), they sought out some humans with whom they could dine.

I've reached the end of the row I'm weeding. It sounds as though the deer has reached the end of its browsing, and it's time to relinquish the shared hour and go our separate ways. But I don't really know what the deer is about to do; even Richard Nelson, author of *Heart and Blood: Living with Deer in America*, admits that "deer have always lingered somewhere beyond my understanding, elusive as moonlight on water. No scientist, no shaman, no stalker, no sentimentalist will ever understand the deer."

I fill a basket with peas and greens and make my way back to the house.

"I WANT TO SEE A COYOTE," I tell poet Jack Haley after a reading at the Shelburne Falls library. He nods, understanding the impulse. He is big-chested and gruff and tender, his poetry full of the war in Vietnam, of family and childhood and different women he has loved.

Over coffee and pastries, he tells me about the winter when he and some friends tracked coyotes with Paul Rezendes at the Quabbin Reservation. They had discovered the trail the first day they were out, just before pitching their tents in the snow, and had followed it all the next day. Three coyotes, they decided, along with a fisher whose trail they lost and a porcupine, which they found in a tree.

On and on they went, finding evidence of coyote kills, of the way coyotes wander, of the places they pause to check out some invisible message. "We locked on them," says Jack. "Of everything we saw that day, they were what fascinated us the most."

The trackers set up camp, digging out places for their tents, heating a meal over small stoves. They picked up the trail again the next morning, noting all the details of coyotes separating, coyotes coming together, coyotes directly registering their prints, intent in their goal.

Then an odd sensation aroused all of them — a familiar scene here, another one there, a curious resemblance to the place where they had started. That's when they got it: they had been led back to their starting place by the coyotes, only now the coyotes were leaving tracks on their tracks. "My God," said Paul, who has spent years studying the ways of animals. "Now they're tracking us."

That's when Jack stops, but I stay caught in the moment, imagining how they must have straightened and turned on their snowshoes, ever so slowly, not knowing if these animals were hungry or commensal. The people checked the trail behind them; they smelled the air in a new way, and then they kept moving, choosing not to linger in a big wilderness in midwinter with the new knowledge of how it feels to be pursued.

A DEER IS IN THE GARDEN, and I don't pause to note how elegant it appears, how red its summer fur is, how much it looks like

my earlier companion. I throw open the door and rush out, yelling. It flees, but in the night it and a smaller deer wander through
the rows and find the chard, the beets, the beans, and, just above
the garden, the new apple trees. They prune terribly, ripping tender branches with each mouthful of leaves. They tromp as much
as they decapitate, leaving baby beets exposed and uprooted slender carrots drying in the sun.

In a box of supplies left by the previous owners, I find a bottle
of "DG-100, All Natural 100% Coyote Urine," and, despite the
reek, I spray it on a dozen small wooden posts and then plant them
carefully around the whole garden.

When my father visits the next day with his two dogs, he can't
figure out what has them so curious and so quick to mark a path as
they pee their way around the field. The bad odor has faded, at
least from a distance.

The next night, a deer is back, undeterred by the range of
smells. More beans are eaten, and the last of that handsome rhubarb chard.

12

I DIVIDE MY TIME between the road and the shadows, the path ahead and the edges it cuts through. The more Holly hurts, the more I hope for a coyote in my line of sight. But on the day of the solstice, it's a fox I drive past, a limp grouse in its mouth. It doesn't want to veer off the pavement and into the woods; the day is too hot, the undergrowth too thick, and in contrast the open road is easy and fast. Its cocked head lets me know it will disappear in a minute, however, if I reduce my speed any further.

I don't. I take the turn into the nearby state forest, park in the lot, and immediately halt, in front of me the bodies of half a dozen moths, the ones with the big wing spots, the lunas and polyphemuses. The lights in the parking lot must draw them for miles, and I imagine a steamy, thrashing night, insects exploding into life and rushing to mate and lay eggs before they die, a frenzy to see who can get to whom the fastest, all around them hungry squirrels, whip-poor-wills, saw-whet owls. When morning comes, the few survivors flutter off to safer places. The others litter the ground, their ragged, bodiless wings strewn like petals.

The scene is similar to that on Maine's offshore islands, the ones occupied by birds that return year after year. They teem with nesting cormorants, eiders, and guillemots, all vying for the same limited territory, raucous and driven and in a constant state of dread or damage. A stench rises like heat waves from dead ducks, torn nests, the bones of chicks that didn't make the dash to the sea but were grabbed instead by hungry gulls, predators that nest on the same outcrops of land. One particular island told of total destruction: a mink had swum over and had a feast to itself, leaping from nest to nest, sucking up eggs like snacks, like hors d'oeuvres, greeting me when I left my kayak as though ready, finally, for company, dashing against my legs, pleased to show off its havoc.

I walk to the lake, which is dark and quiet at this hour, and feel a mix of gladness and dread. I wish I could welcome this day wholeheartedly, content with the arrival of summer, the promise of easy gatherings and generous harvests. But for me the solstice signals the opposite as well, the start of the big slide from now until December. I'm not ready for a decrease in light, even if it's only a minute a day. My time outside already feels too limited; my days inside more compressed and demanding.

Pain has moved into the house, like the crotchety relative neither of us admitted to having, the dependent who has arrived, suitcases and all. Before that, we had such travels together, Holly and I, a joyous momentum that has carried us this far. And then last winter, the first trunk was delivered. I had hung a blanket over the loosest of the windows in an attempt to slow the loss of valuable heat from the house. The day was frigid and short, the sun set at 4:30, and Holly shuddered and turned away from my hammering. "This is how it starts, isn't it?" she asked. "First we shut out the light, then there's the sledding accident, then we can't escape our chairs or our crabbiness, and people we don't like have to feed us."

Six months later, pain's presence is large. I tiptoe so I won't wake it. I move with tenderness and try to look casual. It wants supper; it doesn't. It wants quiet; it needs to stomp. I don't want to hurt its feelings. I don't want to insult it, and I'm worn out because there's no break from its sadness.

For someone who's usually quick to piece together clues, I was slow to understand the series of small changes. Slopes went first, then distances. Pretty soon Holly couldn't get in and out of a car without wincing; now stairs daunt her, even one at a time. She can't put much weight on her right leg, which rules out dancing, bicycling, skipping, leaping, playing hopscotch with small children, or reaching for that thing — keys, a ball, a book — tossed just shy of her arms.

It took a number of awful moments before I realized the implications, like that day we walked together in snow and suddenly she was on the ground because her leg had given out in a long shoot of pain.

I turn away from the quiet water; I can't yet make plans to bring Holly to its shores.

I KNOW NOW why my brother Bob is so fond of his neighbor Danny. He likes Danny's stories — the one about pulling out his own teeth with pliers rather than risking a visit to a dentist, or the one about his father, who, after learning he had cancer, walked into the woods and shot himself in the head, the mess under the trees less to deal with in the long run than what the doctors might have done to his body. It's that straightforward way of assessing pain that attracts Bob; each man — my brother, Danny, Danny's dad when he was living — does a quick calculation of known versus unknown pain, and each grabs for the familiar whenever possible.

I'm more apt to base my decision on trust, except for that time I was fishing with a friend and she buried a lure in my arm. She wanted to push the hook all the way through the skin, cut off the barb, and pull it out (we were out on a lake and she didn't want to go in), but I couldn't bear the idea of it, even though she was good with tools and kept their edges sharp. A slice with a razor-fine knife, a moment's wince, and we'd be able to keep fishing. But I opted for the emergency room, Novocain, stitches, and our relationship ended a short time afterward.

As for Holly, she didn't believe the first specialist who said she'd soon need a new hip. Her body had never failed her; it didn't make sense that it was doing so now. Besides, she was too young; everyone said so. But myriad tests ruled out other diagnoses, and the latest doctor, after examining the new set of x-rays, stated it in a way she could finally hear. "The cartilage is completely gone," he said. "You're walking bone-on-bone. I recommend surgery, as soon as possible."

Soon the ball of her hip will be sawn out and a new unit put in of titanium, Teflon, ceramic, and steel. She'll supply several pints of her own blood beforehand, *just in case*. Then, says the surgeon, a few days in the hospital, a few more in rehab at a nursing home, and a subsequent twelve weeks using crutches or a walker. Three months putting no weight on that leg, no bending at the waist, no turning her foot or crossing her legs. Her bone has to graft onto the new prosthesis, forming a weld that should last twenty years. A fall, of course, could undo the seal; a sudden twist while healing could pop the ball right out.

I distract myself from dread with preparations. I put handrails in the bathroom and pull up the living room rug. I build a cabinet on wheels to house the TV and VCR so we can roll it between rooms. I take off and plane the outside door so it's easy to open and close.

"NOTHING IS SO MUCH to be feared as fear," Thoreau wrote in his journal, though he wasn't describing his own angst in that passage; he was chastising a young writer for not being more forthright in *her* work. The impetus doesn't matter; I know what he means. For me, fear takes root first in my hands, which shake all the time anyway as the result of a benign tremor; but that trembling accelerates when I'm afraid, and I have to jam my hands in my pockets or hang on to my wrists to control it. I can't trust them to keep hold of whatever I've grasped.

But of the several fears I might add to the lone one that Thoreau names, the worst, I think, are the fear of a pain that doesn't cease, the kind that has Holly now, and the fear of despair, the consequence of being unable to do anything about it.

No wonder I want to see the carnivore that lives in dens and dark thickets, the one that thrives despite the myriad assaults against it. Impose fifty-dollar bounties, and its population grows. Increase the number of hunters, and it has larger litters. Send in more sharpshooters, taking aim from helicopters, and the animal begins breeding in its first year of life, rather than waiting until it is closer to two. Coyotes have even figured out how to avoid cyanide bombs, though it's hard to imagine how they sorted that out — the poison is dispersed so fast that death is almost instantaneous.

Yet somehow the survivors — the ones who witnessed the detonation or pieced together the evidence afterward — have figured out the process and learned to avoid the triggers. They store the information, they pass it on, and they just keep traveling, despite the tough odds.

WITH THE WORLD so newly narrowed, I keep my focus close. I don't seek out other people to explore with; I don't go off for hours in the woods; I don't hunt for coyotes, other than in what I read. Instead, I spend way too long in a crouch watching ants ingest a hairless infant squirrel, barely two inches long, left on the driveway near the barn door. I don't know how it landed here; it can't be more than a few hours old, pink and shut-eyed and still fetally curved. Short breaths shake its body and then fade, just before I have to make the decision to end its life fast or let the ants do it slowly.

Another morning I'm again on my knees, amazed at the size of a parasitic worm that squeezed from the anus of a recently dead mouse. I wonder if it will find another host before the ants discover it, though this time I don't wait to witness the outcome.

It's when Chloe begins brushing off small white eggs that jut from the sides of tomato hornworms that I begin to notice how passive I've become around certain forms of pain. I don't tell this sensitive niece that the parasitic wasps that lay these eggs are good for the garden, that they kill the insects that eat the stuff we want. On her face is a clear sense of injustice: the eggs are injuring the fat green caterpillars, and that's an assault she cannot let happen.

WHEN THE STATE wildlife office announces an open forum on the proposed extension of bear-hunting season, I make plans to go, as much for the chance to be in my old high school as for the responses I might hear to this potentially charged topic. With Holly's impending surgery, I have a keener need to know who's around us, beyond our immediate circles of family and friends and coworkers.

People fill the auditorium with a certain resignation. They've been through this process before, most recently with the debates around the Wildlife Protection Act, an acrimonious struggle that resulted in a ban on all leghold traps. Similar struggles have taken place around the country — in Colorado and California, where citizen-sponsored initiatives have sought to ban all leghold or body-gripping traps; in Idaho, Michigan, and Washington, where ballot measures were introduced that would regulate the hunting of bear; and in Maine and Alaska, where voters have worked to end the use of wire snares.

A difficult question associated with each initiative is, who gets to make wildlife policy — the voters or the biologists, whose salaries are paid by both conservationists and sportsmen? But the conflicts tend to get ugliest when "tree-huggers" face off against "murderers." We see it on the local level every time another letter to the editor appears in the paper, with another demand that the Wildlife Protection Act be thrown out and the trapping of coyotes reinstated (*They maul lambs! They take chunks from wounded calves!*). A dissenting letter regularly appears afterward, defending all creatures' rights to unmolested lives and challenging us to examine what we really know about interconnectedness. The only other topics generating as much passion in the press are the pros and cons of the name "Redskins" for the regional high school's athletic teams, and the newspaper's decision to run front-page photographs of the same-sex couples who are suing the state for the right to marry.

But the hunting of bear is the focus tonight, and Jim Cardoza, from MassWildlife, opens the hearing. He begins by describing the change in population, from about 450 bears in 1982, when hunting them was first permitted, to a current high of about 1,800, a growth rate faster than the annual rate of harvest. He talks about ongoing changes in habitat and in citizens' attitudes, about the density of black bear in this area (greater than anywhere else in New England), and then he takes questions, cautiously, before finally stepping back and letting the open-mike time begin.

The room stiffens at the possibility that this could turn ugly.

But the first speakers mostly tell stories: about the bear in a nearby town that developed a taste for marshmallows and tore through a boarded-up porch to get into the house where they were stashed; of the sow and three cubs that wandered through backyards in Pittsfield; of the bear that regularly sits on a front porch in Conway; of the bears in other towns and yards that take out bird feeders and suet cages, small dogs, and stored seed.

The tension begins to mount when some of the farmers step forward, their stories evoking less levity. One man, who plants about 300 acres of corn, says he expects about $1,000 per acre in yield, but the bears are cutting into his slim profits, destroying between six and nine acres each summer. Another man is far more impatient. "The corn's ripe now," he says. "And the bears are going to find it. We need the hunting season backed up even further, from September into August."

Dealing responsibly with this dilemma won't be easy, most of the speakers admit, and fortunately we have several options, including education (train people not to leave bird feeders out in the spring), legislation (make it illegal to feed bear), deterrence (use electric fencing, pepper spray, firecrackers, rubber bullets), and removal and relocation as the last resort.

A certain complacency settles across the room as the comments become more predictable. According to the men, who make up the majority of the 250 or so people present, we have to protect the farmers; we have to protect innocent women and children. We pay for this right to hunt, they say, with our taxes and hunting license fees; we deserve to do it; we ought to be able to say how it's done. And, damn it, we're not Neanderthals.

According to a few women, we need to protect wildlife, not destroy it. We don't need to add to the number of days hunters occupy the woods, all those weeks when neither we nor our children feel safe there. We need to pursue the alternatives more aggressively. "A season on bear deals only accidentally with the ones that pose problems," says one woman. "Killing should be the most extreme, last resort," says another. "Bears have feelings, too," says a third.

"In the woods," one woman sums up, "I'm more afraid of hunters than I am of bear."

A man hurries to the mike to answer her. "If it weren't for the sportsmen, the woods wouldn't be safe for anyone to enter."

I leave the school, wondering where my brothers might stand in such a debate. I like to think they would laugh at the last speaker's belief that he's able to kill off every threat in the woods. I imagine him shooting at snakes and paper wasps' nests, a wild spray of buckshot arcing through the trees. And then I'm hit by the smell of skunk and lose track of everything else. It permeates the parking lot, a stink so sudden and acrid that it seems a fitting end to the idea that any animal population can truly be managed. Bears — big targets that they are — might be herded into small pockets, the way wolves were once driven onto hilltops that were then set on fire. But a species like the skunk, or the coyote, for that matter, will never be corralled or eradicated. We have provided them with too many crannies and hideouts, shaded lays under porches and narrow crawl spaces.

And we have provoked them with too much resistance. For another trait that persists in these hills — one that I enacted in high school when skipping class or agreeing with classmates to forgo the usual yearbook ritual of voting for all those "best" and "most" categories, Vietnam and Kent State making those distinctions feel hollow — is the orneriness that resists being told what to do. It's a memory that heartens me, as does the associated trait, the willingness of neighbors to argue with neighbors, to acknowledge differing opinions in a tightly packed room.

The street lights are too bright for stars to show, but once I'm a few miles out of town, the way home seems somehow clearer and easier than the drive in.

CURIOUS ABOUT other perspectives on the shifting wildlife populations, I talk to Dave Rich, an environmental police officer charged with upholding all the laws of the commonwealth while patrolling remote areas that regular police officers never cover. His days can involve encounters with everything from coyotes and bears and rabid raccoons, to poachers and drug dealers, drunk drivers and nude swimmers and trespassing ATVs.

When I ask if he has seen any change in the number of coyote complaints over the past few years, he tells me first about how short a time the animals have been in this area and what a big deal it was back in the early sixties when he saw a coyote that had been shot in Vermont. (He also remembers what a big deal it was to see his first cardinal, in D.C. in the late fifties, before the bird had started its northward migration.)

Then he acknowledges that the region he covers might be fairly atypical for the state, because the number of coyote hunters keeps the animals fairly furtive; in any case, it's the bear complaints that have completely eclipsed earlier worries about coyotes. He recites a few recent instances: of a bear that killed a woman's ducks; a bear that smashed a plate glass window and entered a living room; a bear that tore up the upholstery of a car for whatever had leaked from grocery bags left on the seat; a bear that went through a cornfield, leaving a bulldozer-sized path. "And it's pretty well documented around here," he says, "that bears have killed goats and calves and sheep and dogs."

What's less well known is the number of people who put food out for them. That worries him. So does the number of resident moose in the state, which now total between three and five hundred. "I don't know where we'll put them all," he says. It's sheer good fortune that there hasn't been a fatality yet in Massachusetts, though there have been plenty of vehicle collisions with moose to the north of us, resulting in many deaths and mutilations.

As for coyotes, he doesn't think their populations have changed much in the last few years, though perhaps there have been more instances of animals afflicted with mange. It's a point that might explain the area's many mountain lion sightings. "You know what people are probably seeing? Coyotes with mange, the hair gone from their tails." It makes sense — a flash of blond coyote slipping into the woods, that thin tail the last thing to be seen. "But think of it this way," he says. "Most people, when you ask them, couldn't tell you a single thing about the bird that just flew by. It might be a blackburnian warbler, but they wouldn't even be able to tell you the size or the color. They're just not used to noticing details about such things, so how do you expect them to recognize the size and shape of a cougar?"

The radio crackles beside him, and he listens a moment before turning down the volume. I look around the park headquarters, a small building not far from the trail where I found a thick hypodermic needle last winter — the remnant of a tranquilizer shot at a bear.

"If you want to see a coyote," he tells me, "a sure way is to listen to the scolding of small birds during fawning season. Find out what they're upset about, and you'll probably find the animal. I heard them doing it this spring. I hunted about, found a fawn, and sure enough, pretty soon I made out the coyote, crouched low in the grass, just waiting to close in on the meal."

The other big change he has seen since the Wildlife Protection Act was passed is the exploding population of beaver. "Their numbers are almost out of control, and the solutions some people are suggesting take way too much time and money. Somebody who's working fulltime can't go out and take apart a beaver dam every day, yet if he doesn't, his land's going to be flooded and he'll lose a lot of timber that, a few years down the road, could have been harvested for good money."

He has also seen an increase in the number of bobcat; he even had a neighbor claim he saw a bobcat take down a deer. Another change — and this one he contemplates carefully before explaining — is that rabies used to come in cycles, "with a significant outbreak about every twenty-five to thirty years. Now, though, there seems to be an outbreak every year, especially in the spring when raccoons come out of their dens. It's what they call the 'dumb strain,' perhaps because a raccoon's eyes glaze over and it stumbles around, looking fairly stupid. Though when skunks get it, it's awful. They squeal and run around in circles as though they're in incredible pain. Sometimes you'll find them with porcupine quills in them, too, which is a good sign that they've probably been infected that way."

I could listen far longer to his stories, gathered from sixty-plus years of observing everything that moved in the woods — how in winter the presence of coyotes is obvious when deer move close to houses, or how mink climb trees in pursuit of squirrels, or how coyotes cache food. But he has work to do, another few miles to patrol, and the possibility, he's just been told, that someone may be illegally harvesting timber from nearby state land.

13

IT'S OVER. The old hip has been removed, the new one inserted. We're no longer limited to our imaginations and our stories; we can resume physical activity in the world once again. Though first I have to figure out how to occupy the house, and I'm close to tears when a phone call interrupts me. "Is she okay?" my brother Bob asks. "Want me to do anything?"

I want him to understand everything, all at once, especially how hard it is to be the strong one all the time. "They removed the epidural, tried to get her out of bed, and she almost hit the floor. And if she falls and the joint pops out, they'll have to cut her open and do this all again." I've left her in the hospital, tubed and wired, so I can sleep for a few hours. But our house still smells from last night's fight under the porch, a row that jarred me awake, the scent of angry skunk steaming through immediately after. I've opened doors, I've turned on fans, but I know I can't bring her home to this.

"She'll feel trapped," I tell him. "She won't be able to get away from it."

"It'll be gone in a few days," he says, "and if it isn't, I'll get you an industrial-size fan, and we'll blow out everything that isn't nailed down."

Tenderness swells through me, and I can see him in the photograph I once took, a tall man tilting to the side so he could hold his small daughter's hand as they walked through a field. I tell him how much Holly still hurts and how hard it is to see her strapped and dependent, but my eyes are tearing. "The stink's burning the air," I say, so he won't know how his call has affected me, or how it comes after a whole string of such moments, beginning with my parents, who arrived to be by Holly's bedside when she was just waking from surgery.

His voice says he understands that this, right now, is the worst fear of all, that if something happened to Holly, I'd be emptied of joy, that even letting in that thought hurts more than I can admit, and I want to bang around, slam doors, find the skunk, find an out.

And have my big brother take care of me, if only for a few hours.

"Skunks used to wander into the barn," he says of the place where he lived with his first wife, "and then the sheep would thunder in and startle them. And they'd spray, and you couldn't get away from it. It'd be in our eyes, our clothes; everyone would be hurting."

He pauses, and I pin the phone under my chin and pour myself a glass of wine.

"You know what you have to do," he says, and I hear him pick up speed as he paces through his house. "You've got to get yourself a gun. That's the quickest way to deal with them. I used to shoot them right there in the barn, or follow them outside and nail them in the field." His voice swells with new energy. "It's the only way to get rid of them. The longer you let them stay, the more they'll feel welcome. Shoot them now, or it'll get worse when they start spinning off more babies."

But I don't want a gun. I don't want to shoot them. I want Holly to stop hurting. I want her home, I want her strong, I want her well. "We'll be fine," I say, and he tells me to call him if I think of anything he can do.

"A fan," he says. "Just say the word and I'll bring you a fan."

I hang up and remember the time he and his three sons visited us in D.C., when we lived near Dupont Circle, around men holding hands, women tight with women, and he wanted us to know about his lesbian friend, the woman who, he claimed, had saved his life when a wasp sting almost stopped his heart, and how he hoped he'd live long enough to do something as big for her.

I want to do something that big, too, though this is all so incremental, one hour at a time, another night to get through. I finish the wine, grab a sleeping bag, and move outside to sleep.

DAYS LATER, Holly is home, the nursing home fading like a bad dream. With sleep about to take her down again, she barely asks the question before her eyes close. "Will you love my new seam as much as you loved my old leg?"

I wish I could cradle her close. But too many recent images crowd between us — her legs strapped inside a fat wedge of blue foam; an IV in one arm, an epidural in her back; the terror in her face when the old pain seemed not to have abated. I brush hair from her forehead and temples; I stroke her head and arms. I want an end to spending nights as loose as a leaf blown between waking and sleep. The thump-drag of the walker, and I'm instantly alert; the subsequent calm, and I drift along darkness.

My old bicycling gloves have helped pad her palms, and calluses have formed from all that shuffling of the walker, but the bike basket didn't work as an attachment, and so she tied what she needed to the walker itself — the long-handled gripper, the portable phone, a cloth sack with a bottle of water. At night, particularly, she sounds like a peddler clanging her wares, and I feel each clump-hop through the floor as she travels from bedroom to bathroom to kitchen and back.

Meanwhile, I do the carrying. Groceries, meals, laundry; books, mail, towels; the cup of coffee she can't move from the kitchen to the couch; the glass of water to wash down some more pills. I stay present without seeming obvious, like watching a bird or animal without making eye contact because to do so would send it skittering away. I take brief naps; I'm quickly in and out of the shower. I hold on to no thought longer than a sentence.

The evening when it seems we've settled into a rhythm at last, I pick up Barry Lopez's *Of Wolves and Men* and begin flipping pages, starting at the back. The photo I come upon is both soothing and compelling — a mosaic depicting a tree, a wolf, and two small children who appear to be dancing beneath her. Nothing about the image invokes *wolf*, however; her face is wide-eyed and passive, her posture that of a large horse. She's the "benevolent wolf mother," runs the caption, with "Romulus and Remus."

The rest of the chapter describes Lopez's search for some kind of mythic or literary tradition of "wolves who nurture," though he finds little that's positive in the histories of werewolves, of feral men, of souls of different sorts trapped in the bodies of wolves. "But I think," he writes, "that looking for the wolf-mother is the stage we are at now in history . . . [W]hether out of guilt or because we have reached such a level of civilization as to allow us the thought, we are looking for a new wolf. We seem eager to be corrected, to know how wrong our ideas about wolves have been, how complex the creature really is, how ultimately unfathomable." He ends the passage with a paraphrase from Henry Beston about animals not being "brethren" or "underlings," but "other nations, caught with ourselves in the web of life."

What he says about wolves could apply to coyotes as well. In attitudes I heard at the hearing on bear hunting, in stories students have told me, in feelings shared by friends and neighbors and various family members, I hear a gathering readiness, albeit sometimes reluctant, for a new interpretation of this artful, omniscient predator.

Holly sleeps on, and I pick up another article, describing a behavioral difference that's showing up between eastern and western coyotes. Scientists studying the play behavior of coyote pups have found that, overall, eastern coyotes are more playful than their western cousins of the same age. They're also less aggressive and less apt to signal their interest in play, which means that instead of asking, Will you play with me? they just launch into the act. They wrestle, they chase, they nip, they pin, until the one on the bottom escapes, and the game starts all over again.

For western coyotes, which have lived in a hostile environment far longer than eastern coyotes have, signaling play is more prevalent, perhaps as a kind of coping mechanism when the very act of play may keep a pup from sensing danger. According to the study, western pups signal a desire to play 90 percent of the time, while eastern coyotes make such signals only a third of the time. Another possibility, the author suggests, in addition to the East being a less hostile place, is that this impulse to play may be part of that genetic package inherited from wolves, which, researchers have found, are even more playful than eastern coyotes.

It's a fascinating concept, especially here in the heart of staid New England. The new arrival is not only a larger and more sociable animal than its western counterpart, but it's also more likely to break into spontaneous play.

Wit, I presume, is also part of the new package, a trait Larry Engel captures in a story he tells about a coyote he tried to film for his television documentary *Wild Tales About America's Top Dogs*. In an article in *National Wildlife*, he describes the difficulty in getting close enough to film a coyote in Yellowstone National Park. Fortunately, when Curly Bear Wagner arrived (a local Blackfoot tribal elder), so did a coyote — within fifty yards of the film crew.

"We circled around to try to get images of the animal," Engels is quoted as saying. "Then someone shouted, 'He's circling back toward us!' Sure enough, the coyote walked to within twenty feet of Curly Bear. I was so excited to get this footage. But when I got back to the studio, I discovered that in all the feet of film we shot, this was the only sequence with a defect in it, making it unusable."

My eyelids sag, but I don't want to end this chance to think my own thoughts, to sort out and embellish as my imagination sees fit. I pull out one more article, this one about Stuart Ellins's work in California and his attempts to figure out how coyotes communicate.

In a simple experiment with the coyotes he'd been raising, Ellins separated the animals into two different kennels. He then fed sheep meat to both groups, though one of them received meat laced with lithium. The coyotes eating the tainted meat got miserably sick while the others had no reason to distrust their meal. Then he put the animals together in one enclosure, the coyotes that had been poisoned with the coyotes that hadn't, and somehow, through some language he hasn't yet figured out, a flare in pheromones perhaps, or some undetected change in behavior, the message was relayed — *Don't touch that stuff!* — and almost immediately none of the coyotes would eat sheep again.

Ellins's goal is a good one: he wants coyotes to warn each other about certain kinds of meat (sheep, cats) before they develop a taste for livestock or domestic pets. Yet right now, I wouldn't mind if no one ever figured out how such messages travel, fast and invisible and utterly necessary.

I stumble up from the chair to check on Holly one last time and find her fast asleep, the sheet tangled by her feet. Careful not to wake her, I pull the thin cover up over her bandaged body. Her fingers twitch as though she knows, as though she hears all that my body is saying, and her hand stretches out and sleep-strokes my arm.

14

I STASH THE LAST of the semester's work, look up, and see a slip of white paper blowing through the trees. Only it isn't trash, and there's no wind. It's a short-tailed weasel in its phase of ermine white, a sign of winter readiness in a brown and naked wood. The ermine's speed is surely related to how vulnerable it looks, the stark contrast of white against shreds of bark and rotting leaves.

Westward, out the same window, a ruffed grouse pick its way along the rock wall. Within a few minutes, a red-tailed hawk lands in the tallest sugar maple, a drama set to unfold. But the grouse has stalled, the hawk can't detect it against the look-alike leaves, and eventually it soars on. Had the grouse blinked or twitched, the hawk would have had an easy meal.

The weasel's white against brown, the grouse's dark camouflage saving it from death, and, so far, a snowless winter when a grouse can hide and a weasel can't: nothing seems quite right about the season. If the snows don't come soon and the temperature does drop, as it's bound to do at least once in January, the grouse won't have its shelter of drifts to dig into at night, no insulation to keep hypothermia at bay. And that ermine, one of the fiercest of all the predators for its size, will continue to be as obvious as a swan on a dark lake.

It's not clear where that leaves them — a fat grouse needing another kind of shelter, an ermine ahead in the setting of its clock. Perhaps only an evolutionary leap to a single year-round pelt will save the weasel. Either that or its territory will have to recede into northern lands where snow is still a part of every winter, and thick white hoar provides a screen through which to view the world.

But who or what would want to plod north, to leave this light and move closer to the Arctic Circle, where sunlight wanes almost as fast as water freezes? The nine hours we're reduced to on the shortest days of the year would seem rich in contrast to the two, then one, then none farther north. And yet that's exactly what coyotes did, trudging ever northward as they moved out of the Southwest. They went from intensely bright, arid days to dark, deep-snowed cold. They adapted to the extremes of deserts and boreal forests, moving from the great expanses of Big Sky Country to the closed-in, hatched networks of woods and towns of the rural Northeast. Not only did they adjust to wide fluctuations in light and temperature and rainfall, they also accommodated all those different insects and snakes and briars and traps, along with highways and railways, fences and culverts, dams and bridges and sewer pipes. And still they keep heading north.

Meanwhile, on this particular curve of earth, the winter solstice has come and gone, and each day or so the sun provides another minute of light. It's the annual signal — another corner rounded, from darkness to light, hard times to a day full of promise.

ANOTHER ODDLY MILD January day. Ice whiskers in the path have begun to collapse, leaving stretches of path slick with melt. The sun barely clears the ridge, even at the height of day, and most of the river stays in shadow. On a high point of the trail, I find a calf carcass in an awkward sprawl of stiff legs and muddy hair, an obvious lure to coyote scavengers that might slink within rifle range.

I can't tell if the bait worked. I see no shells or scuffed leaves, no signs of struggle or blood. For that matter, I see little life around me. No hunters, no animals, and only a few birds. But I stay attentive, as hunting season is now open on almost every animal but bear and deer, and what I uncovered while reading up on the hunting laws — especially those in New Hampshire — did little to reassure me about some of the people taking to the woods at this time of year.

Of all the northeastern states, Massachusetts has the shortest hunting season on coyotes; currently it lasts only two months, though soon that will double in length, from the beginning of November to the end of February. In Vermont, coyotes can be shot at any time of year, as they can in Rhode Island and in Maine. Maine also employs the most controversial coyote-control program in the region. It advocates the use of snares and, in contrast to the laws governing the use of other trapping devices, these traps — consisting of a wire loop through which a coyote sticks its head and a washer that locks down and keeps the cable from loosening — don't have to be checked every few days; trappers can go up to a week without inspecting them. An antisnare group in Maine has pointed out that this causes a cruel, protracted death, often resulting in animals with "jellyhead" (swollen and soft from the myriad ruptured vessels) or in animals that don't die but have to wait seven days for the trapper to arrive and finish the job. They also maintain that, since coyotes are presenting no clear threat to livestock or deer populations, such an aggressive damage control program puts Maine out of step with most contemporary management plans. But the fact that these snares pose a threat to the endangered Canada lynx may supply the one reason strong enough to reverse the practice.

Elsewhere in the Northeast, Connecticut closes its coyote season for only five weeks a year (three weeks in May and two weeks in October), while the season in New York runs for six months, from the beginning of October until the end of March, with no bag limits and no distinctions made between hunting at night or during the day. New Hampshire has the most liberal and specific laws regarding coyotes. They may be hunted or trapped year-round, and they may be hunted at night from January to

March. Lights may be used, except those from cars or off-road vehicles, and electronic coyote callers are permissible, though it's illegal to bait on ice-covered waterways. Curiously, New Hampshire lawmakers have also felt it necessary to spell out a statute others might think is obvious. Number one under their General Hunting Laws clearly states, "It is unlawful to negligently shoot, wound or kill a human being while hunting, or abandon a wounded or killed human being."

After another hour of walking, I leave the trail when it veers from the river; I want to stay near the water, though it's tough going through the tight weave of red osier and young willow. But the rhythm of the river and evidence of recent beaver activity are having a good effect on me. And then I find the lodge, a jumble of mud and sticks tucked against the bank on sand swept clean by recent rain.

I wonder if beaver wake when someone walks on their roof, whether they sense a coyote circling outside or know that coyotes increasingly look on them as food. It's another sign of the changes the eastern coyote is making, or so suggests Henry Hilton, who has been studying beaver for many years in Maine. Recently, he has started seeing evidence of coyotes that have investigated active beaver trails or bedded down near the holes beavers make in spring ice. He suspects coyotes may have developed a "search image" for beaver, a way to recognize prey that for years they typically ignored, though he also suspects that hunting beaver might be a behavioral trait they inherited from wolves — more possible evidence of the mixing of genetic instructions.

Of course, it might also be something coyotes learned through paying careful attention to their surroundings. Ray Coppinger has found that coyotes are excellent "observational learners," and he illustrates that fact with a series of anecdotes from the time when he raised coyote pups along with border collies. It took him a while to realize that the coyotes could escape from their kennel and that they had been doing so for quite some time. (He spread flour around the buildings to confirm his suspicions, the giveaway footprints telling the story in the morning.) "Every night they were out in the field by the kennel hunting mice. Why didn't the border collies watch and learn how to get out? Why did the coyotes come back? . . . The important point," he writes in *Dogs: A Startling New Understanding of Canine Origin, Behavior and Evolution*, which he coauthored with his wife, Lorna, "is . . . that not only were the wild animals better at solving a problem [than the collies], but they learned how to solve a problem by watching another animal, including humans."

As I circle this beaver lodge, I wish we as Europeans in the New World were better observational learners, particularly of the native peoples who once roamed this area. The trail I took to get here is part of a network of paths that people have been traveling for over 10,000 years. This particular trail connected the Connecticut River to the Hudson Valley, and a nearby natural waterfall was a popular place to fish. Tribes that camped here honored a local peace treaty, or so the story goes, so they could concentrate on gathering the shad and salmon thrashing upriver on their annual spring run. I can imagine the encampments, an easy sprawl of tepees and cooking fires and fish-drying racks, and the chance to trade goods and tales with others.

One such story might have been that of the giant beaver that lived in these parts, precursor to the one that might be near me right now, only it weighed between 600 and 700 pounds, with incisors that extended four inches from its gums. As Mashilik, an elderly Pocumtuck woman, told the story (collected by Kathleen Abbott in her 1907 book *Old Paths and Legends of the New England Border*), this giant beaver lived in a huge nearby lake — presumably the glacial lake that filled the Connecticut River valley until some 12,000 years ago — and tormented other animals whenever he rose from the water. Mighty Hobomuck, protector of the lesser creatures, finally decided the dangerous beaver should die, and he struck it across the shoulders with a stout oak club. The beaver sank to the bottom and turned into stone; years later, the petrified body emerged as the lake receded, the geological formation known today as Mt. Sugarloaf.

The implications of such a story could realign all our paradigms, for the very notion that a word-of-mouth transmission may have endured for 12,000 years makes our historical traditions seem impoverished in comparison. The stories I grew up with aren't even half as old — the Biblical stories of Noah and Abraham may go back 5,000 years, while the great epics of the Western canon, the *Iliad*, the *Odyssey*, date to about 3,000 years before the present. The story of the giant beaver and the glacial lake, both of which took scientists until the nineteenth century to explain, puts oral traditions in a whole new light.

COYOTE SCAT, in three discrete piles, snaps me out of my thinking as fast as though I'd heard the animal howl. It's in the middle of the trail and looks deliberately arranged.

I don't need calipers to confirm the source, though a more serious tracker might whip them out. I calculate width by using the distance between joints on my right index finger (one and a quarter inches), one of the few body measurements I know (along with the eight-inch stretch between my thumb and middle finger and the five-foot length of my pace on level ground). These droppings easily pass the coyote test. It's the narrower scats, closer to an inch in width, that can't be distinguished from that of a fox, and in those instances I look for other clues.

In *A Field Guide to Animal Tracks*, a book I learned to depend on as a child, Olaus Murie warns of the difficulties in trying to distinguish fox from coyote scat, but he was writing before the coyote moved east and picked up its wolf genes and enlarged everything about itself. Paul Rezendes, who has been measuring scat width for years, writes that the eastern coyote's is consistently thicker than a fox's. It's also potentially dangerous. Like the scat of many animals, it can contain eggs of two different tapeworm parasites, which, when they hatch in humans, can be fatal. The eggs of the roundworm also pose a problem, as the larvae travel erratically in the body and become adults wherever they land.

I'm careful, and this time I bring none of the evidence home.

Instead, in this dry air, I practice my sense of smell, which is poor. An expert tracker might walk these same woods and sniff out scent posts and piss patches and know whose territory she's on or what animal has recently passed by. Occasionally I've picked out the rancid odor of raccoon or the acrid pee of cats. But for the most part, the naming of smells eludes me. Holly can sniff bread and list the herbs, catch a perfume and name the brand and the year it was fashionable. I'm lucky if I get the right category — foods, bodies, machines, flowers, clam flats, swamps, oak woods. I confuse narcissus with hot wires, violets with lilac, certain soaps with the grandparents who died when I was a child.

The only smell I pick up now is rank air, January air, with little moisture in it and no hint of snow. I could take advantage of this open winter and set out a board when I get home, as I learned from another Murie book. Set out live traps, he wrote, to capture the littlest of the rodents, and place a board near a traveled path for the larger mammals to mark. They can't resist depositing their scat on it. And I remember a story Jack Haley told me, of a hike he and some friends took around the Quabbin Reservoir. They had stopped for lunch, spreading out on the rocks overlooking a big stretch of valley. Then something pulled them away, after they'd eaten and sunned and rested, and when they returned to collect their packs, they found fresh coyote scat on the very spot where they had sat just minutes before.

15

"IF YOU WANT to see coyotes," people tell me, "go to the Quabbin Reservoir in the dead of winter. If any deer are down on the ice, coyotes will be there to clean them up."

It makes sense, as some of the best photographs I have seen of coyotes were taken at the Quabbin in winter. It seems paradoxical, but the deer, whose smooth hooves are unable to get traction on ice, are attracted to it when the surrounding land is covered with thick snow. Given a choice between wading through thigh-deep powder or crossing a hard surface that might have been roughened by wind and freeze-thaw patterns, the deer invariably choose the latter. Ice can even supply them with an advantage against a predator such as a wolf or coyote. If the deer can get enough purchase, it can kick out and inflict considerable damage on a canid that comes too close, another reason that coyotes are reluctant to try to take down a healthy buck or doe. In deep snow, however, the advantage rests with the coyote if it also has the patience to outlast the deer, which are ill equipped to defend themselves under such conditions. With the bitter cold that has descended on us at last, the chances are good that the water's surface will be frozen, that deer may have wandered out, and that some of them will have gotten into trouble.

On a map, the Quabbin Reservoir is easily the largest body of freshwater in the state and the fourth largest of any of New England's lakes, "a slaphazard streak of blue," writes Thomas Conuel in *Quabbin: The Accidental Wilderness*, "a child's finger-painting across the face of central Massachusetts." A long strip of land, Prescott Peninsula, separates the two blue streaks. Though the peninsula is closed to the public, I toured it one winter with a wildlife biology class as part of a study of grouse and deer habitats. Its remoteness adds to its rich variety of wildlife, making it an ideal classroom for all kinds of ecological pursuits.

In today's cold, however, little will be active, though the views should be fine in this clear air. I invite Holly to come with me for the sights and the chance to test her hip under such conditions.

We layer. We stop on the way for doughnuts and coffee, cheap heat that can't last very long. An hour later, we park on a hill overlooking the water. From here, the reservoir looks more like an ocean than an inland lake, dark and laced with whitecaps and more vast than I remember, stretching over fifteen miles away from where we sit in the car, the heater on as high as it will go. From this vantage point, it's easy to see why the site was chosen for the "great land grab," as people in the western part of the state call it, the direct consequence of being near an urban area that coveted its river and sharply defined valley. Boston had to find a reliable resource to quench the thirst of its growing population, and they chose the Swift River, surrounded by four towns so small they could offer little political resistance.

It didn't take too much effort, as relocation programs go, to move those twenty-five hundred people — the ones farming, hunting, fishing, logging, or working at one of the local mills, making boxes, soapstone foot warmers, palm-leaf hats, or Shaker bonnets, all those people receiving word that their town would soon be flooded. The Depression was on, property values had plummeted, and protest, ultimately, was brief. Mostly, the displaced residents packed their favorite possessions, sold off what they could to eager, out-of-state collectors, loaded up the memories that could travel, and moved to safer ground.

It's the place-bound memories that couldn't be shifted, the ones that still linger somewhere under the water. Little physical evidence remains of the life of a town — all the houses from Dana, Enfield, Prescott, and Greenwich were moved or razed, the factories were demolished, and the bodies from thirty-four cemeteries were reinterred elsewhere (though the Native American graves were left behind to be flooded). Yet it's hard to look over this vast body of water and not think about those who once lived there — the kids attending school, people out in the fields, others gathering to talk on the way to the market.

Old photographs document the process: beginning in 1928, the hillsides were stripped of trees, homes, churches, and barns, and scraped clean with earthmoving machines. Little was left but stone walls and glacial erratics. (Though some buildings, like the Enfield Town Hall, stayed standing until 1939. About three thousand people attended the last event held there — a dance to commemorate its closing — and wept during the moment of silence at evening's end, knowing that their town had just ceased to exist. The earthen dam that closed off the narrow end of the valley had been completed, though it took another seven years for the reservoir to fill.) By the end of World War II, clear, clean water was flowing through an aqueduct to Boston from the largest body of untreated drinking water in the world.

It's a stunning creation, with over 25,000 acres of water and over 50,000 acres of wilderness, most of it forested and rich in bird and animal life. It's also a fabulous example of the cycle of land use, from wooded to cleared and back to wooded again, forming what cartographer Christopher Ryan describes in his map of the reservation as a "sanctuary for all . . . those people who seek relief from the daily stress of artificial and congested environments." It is also a wildlife refuge, and an angler's haven for trout and bass and landlocked salmon, a place where moose have strengthened their numbers, and claims have been made about mountain lion sightings.

Today, in this bitter air, the water steams, while the wind stirs it too violently for ice to form. No deer will wander from the cover of trees; no coyote will risk revealing itself. We leave the car carefully and take to the woods for the tracks and the relative quiet. Around us is evidence of the once-farmed land — old stone walls, apple trees ringing visible cellarholes, and a mixed-age, mixed-growth forest. The size of the deer population is obvious from the distinct browse line on the trees, branches pruned as high as a deer can reach. Such clearing out of the under-growth should make it easy to see considerable distances through the woods. It's the wind that makes it hard; my eyes can't stop tearing.

"I think I might lose my eyebrows," Holly says, though talking is tricky, all that warmth escaping each time we open our mouths, the wind chill reported to be about −40° F. "My eye sockets are shrinking," she announces a few minutes later.

Down by the water, ring-billed gulls lift and drop in the gusts, mergansers ride out the crests, and a lone bald eagle drifts overhead. Yet despite the quick freeze of tears on our eyelashes and the frost that forms on the scarves around our faces, there will be no ice on the water today. There is plenty alongside it, however. Thick-frosted rocks and wind-carved hoar sculptures have transformed the length of the southern shore from jagged and guarded to white-humped and soft.

Eventually we head for the visitor's center to thaw out. "Ah," says the volunteer working inside, "you can never count on seeing ice on the reservoir. The whole thing has frozen over only half of the winters since it was created."

That means there will be no easy, predictable way to see a coyote. Crossing paths will be pure chance, as in the story our friend Grace recently told of a night when she was driving a visitor back from the airport, and the friend wanted to know what a coyote looked like. The resulting coincidence was uncanny, as Grace turned her head and pointed. "Like that," she said, of the animal that had just appeared on the side of the busy road.

ON THE WAY HOME, we stop by Holly's office and pick up a kitten, a small, long-haired calico with a Maine coon's features. A coworker can no longer keep it, and she doesn't want to take it to an animal shelter.

It makes no sense at all for us to claim her — we've heard another report of a missing cat in the neighborhood, with conflicting stories about whether it was taken by a coyote or a bobcat. But another warm body in the house seems like a good idea to both of us, another sign of domesticity, more proof that we're planning to stay. We fit her into a box and head back to the car.

She's almost strong enough to push up the box flaps that I'm holding down, though I stretch both arms across the top and press the box to my lap. That's when I know she's too wild to be an indoor cat, too willful to be docile or contained. I like the ferocity, even when I start to feel the seepage of fast-cooling liquid, pee that soaks through all the layers — the cardboard, my jeans, my long underwear.

THE SNOW IS NEW AND SOFT, and I wander on snowshoes along the edge of the field. So had a small canid, accompanied by a larger one, though I can't be sure if they're foxes or coyotes. What is clear is that they traveled along the frozen brook, which is covered with a dusting of snow and is low and secretive in contrast with its higher banks.

I follow the prints around hummocks and over rocks and then reach a small clearing under the pines, where the ground is littered with tracks and packed snow, as though they had wrestled and rolled in a great burst of play.

Or a great burst of foreplay. This is, after all, mating season for both foxes and coyotes, with early February the ideal time to come together. I feel stunned by the proximity. This site is less than one hundred yards from the studio where I spent so much time last summer, hoping for the sight of a coyote out the window. Though the snow is too scuffed to know for sure, I imagine they were tied for at least the half hour needed for fertilization — their tracks, after all, had been so close on the way over, with no move to attempt the direct registering that requires one to follow behind the other. They hightailed it to this site, and then they were all over each other.

I step backward, looking around for other clues. Then I see the den's entrance on the opposite slope above the brook, made obvious by the fresh dirt prints staining the clean snow around it. Tracks from several directions lead toward it, and I can hardly contain my pleasure. An active den, this close to the house.

Keeping my distance — I don't want to deter them by bringing my scent too close — I make the calculations. Both coyotes and foxes tend to establish a den right after mating, though they don't necessarily occupy it until whelping begins. The coyote's gestation is longer, roughly sixty-three days to the fox's fifty-three. If I'm reading this right, the fox kits would be born during my March vacation from school, while if they're coyotes, they'll arrive closer to April Fool's Day. Another three to four weeks will have to pass before the young are active outside the den, and I wonder if I'll know any more by then.

A few days later, I again slip on snowshoes, though I have little time before dark and too much overdue schoolwork. But the den beckons me out of the house, as does the abundance of tracks. From the old pasture, I enter the woods on a narrow trail I hadn't seen before, the path the deer must take to reach our garden. It's quiet here; the trees press close.

I disturb an owl that doesn't want to fly far, though several chickadees protest, and three crows burst into brief noise. In the sumac-bittersweet clearing, I watch a flock of thirty or so robins feed on red berries. Small breast feathers, so pale they're almost pink, have caught inside the imprint of cat tracks, presumably the predator that fed on fresh bird. Farther on I find tracks that I'm sure must be a coyote's — oval-shaped and about two and a half inches wide, with the print of the middle two nails appearing close together (a dog's print is rounder, its nails farther apart). Then I find scat that is clearly a coyote's; the bone chips are too large for a fox, whose jaws aren't strong enough to break the bones of deer, and it's almost black — a sure sign that the animal has eaten fresh meat. It's probable that a carcass is somewhere nearby, perhaps the remains of the deer that visited us last year. Yet it's houses I'm suddenly aware of seeing, not a lump of deer remains; more specifically, it's the lights of house after house visible through the trees, and here I am, passing, as do the deer and coyote, foxes and bobcats, unheard and unseen by the nearby residents.

I'm struck again by how often our backs are turned to these scenes. We orient toward the road, the downslope to town, the way to work and school and shops and friends, while foxes and coyotes slip by, and deer, their hair so dark this time of year it looks wet. It's deer spoor that's most abundant here, more evidence that they're present far more often than we notice.

The year I canoed the Connecticut River from the Canadian border down to Long Island Sound, I had this same sense of looking at the backsides of houses and towns. All dwellings and businesses were turned away from the river in favor of promises beckoning from elsewhere, and the two of us in our canoe, a puppy between us, were not much larger than a floating log. Our days often felt secretive and primal — when the waters were clean we bathed naked and feasted on fiddleheads; we floated past moose and great blue herons; we watched the courtship of loons and the lively fishing of otter.

At other times we drifted in waves of nostalgia, the miles taking us through a history of waste and abandonment. We paddled over the stone walls and barbed wire fences of flooded farmland; we passed steep trash banks of half-buried appliances; we hurried out of reach of pipes spewing foul-smelling, bizarrely colored effluents. The contrast became most apparent when, having seen no one all morning, we rounded a curve and there was the city of

Hartford, straight ahead of us. (We had as little preparation for some of the unmarked dams, when we had to hie for the closest shore before the pull of falling water took hold.) We saw only a few old men as we passed, fishing near broken piers or resting under bridges. Everyone else was invisible and contained.

It was the late seventies, and people were busy rebuilding their lives after a tumultuous decade. The Clean Water Act was still a new measure with no muscle; pride in the river was still decades away. I don't think I'd have believed the optimist who predicted that the Connecticut would become an "American Heritage River," its water rated Class B (fishable and swimmable), and in a few places Class A (drinkable). Nor would I have believed it if someone had predicted that coyotes would soon live in such numbers among us.

When we paddled the river, coyotes had already been in New England for twenty or so years, yet despite the ideal habitat provided by the thickets lining the river, we saw no sign of them. Three weeks and 410 miles, spent almost completely outside or under the thin skin of a tent, and we never heard or caught a glimpse of one.

We did, however, learn quite a bit about a coyote relative, the six-month-old malamute puppy traveling with us. We were told that the breed doesn't swim, which meant we were stuck with her in the boat, at risk whenever she started that rapid shift from side to side, particularly where the warm water around power plants produced carp so fat they roiled the shallows, tantalizing and huge and just out of her reach. But after a few days of near misses, she flew off the bow into a churn of fast water, and though she wailed and splashed, we kept paddling. She swam and was good at it, and when she headed for shore, she proved to be equally good at racing along the water's edge, keeping pace with our canoe. Once we figured out how to tire her, the trip went more smoothly, except for the times something distracted her and she forgot to keep up; or the nights she treed a raccoon outside the tent and barked for it to come down; or that time she found a piece of old meat. I told her to drop it, and she refused. I grabbed for it, and in an instant she transformed into a wolf-self I hadn't seen before, with a fierce, teeth-bared grip on the dead animal, her eyes and growl letting me know she'd go for my hand or arm, maybe my throat, if I didn't back off.

That's where the memory ends. I don't remember what happened next, whether I left her to find us later, or whether I asserted my dominant role, flung the meat, and pulled her back to the canoe. (I should have known what to do, having read all of Jack London's books as a kid.) It's far easier to call up the times she would ride in my daypack when we were cross-country skiing and she could no longer keep up, or when she'd press against my legs in her eager morning greeting, or that time she howled outside a diner that had a no-dogs policy, and a waitress tossed her a bone that kept her quiet until we finished eating. But that image of sudden ferocity, of the fact that she would have bitten my hand had I

messed with her food, has remained the most vivid of the many
I've saved of her.

Somehow it seems connected with my desire to see a coyote,
with my need to walk to the field in the dark and listen for their
sounds.

16

Two of my coworkers have just given birth, two others have announced pregnancies, and a new-baby joy suffuses each woman. Yet though I take turns cradling the new infants and attend showers for those still unborn, it's the new litter in the den on the hill that I find myself drawn to most strongly. It's their heartbeats I want to hear, their whimperings and nuzzlings and slurpy nursing sounds.

It's a desire I don't want to reveal to anyone, not even to Holly, as though it might expose some musky, antisocial streak in me. I'd prefer to think it's all the unknowns about a delivery in the wild that have attracted me. Yet I suspect that it's something far more primitive, some subconscious belief in having the power to create reality, that my desire to see a coyote has somehow brought them this close.

On an afternoon when I arrive home early from school, I make a wide loop through the woods so I can watch the den entrance obliquely. Nothing moves, and eventually I pass to the far side of the hill. The dark tree trunks are encircled by widening areas of melt, every small hollow is full of active snow fleas, and on the limbs above, chickadees whistle their two-noted call. And then, once again, I find dirty canid footprints crossing the white snow, though they don't come from the direction of the original den. I have stumbled onto a second burrow, also with a mound of new dirt in front, made by an animal determined to enlarge it.

These tracks, freshly made and defined by loose soil, seem smaller than a coyote's, however. With the tape measure that now travels in my pocket, I check the widths of several prints; the results suggest a large fox, no matter how many tracks I measure. I choose not to run the tape across the den entrance, which could be as narrow as seven or eight inches and still accommodate a fox's fast dive. I don't want my scent to dissuade the potential tenants from their choice of home.

Shortly afterward, I ask Paul Rezendes what it might mean that two active dens are so close to each other, whether it signals two different families or, better yet, the possibility that one is a fox's, the other a coyote's. Paul studies me for a moment before answering, his face quiet but for his intense eyes. He's shy, I've been told; he'd rather be in the woods than meeting new people; but helping others decipher stories found in sand and mud and snow matters to him, and so he attends events at regularly scheduled intervals, and he spends time talking with people like me.

We stand overlooking a lake where otters have traveled, their fishy-smelling scat on the small peninsula very near us. "Having several dens is typical of foxes," Paul says, "though it's also true of coyotes. And it's pretty common for them to move the young from one den to the other." He smiles, presumably with the pleasure of their cunning. "Then again, the dens might also be connected through a system of underground tunnels."

So the mystery is still mine to solve. While I'm at it, however, I ask whether a fox might take a swing at an opossum, as there were spots of blood in the tracks of an opossum that had passed close to the den and gone up through our yard. But Paul can't tell me the answer. "We know very little about how foxes and opossums interact," he says. "The opossum is still too new here." And then, ever the teacher, he points out that an otter's scat is so acidic it turns the grass below it black, and that it always contains plenty of fish scales.

WITH THE FADING OF SNOW, the force for mating becomes more obvious, most recently in the male turkey that strutted in a nearby field, puffed to twice his normal size, his wattle aflame, his tail feathers fanned. He was oblivious to people, cars, the noises from the neighboring house. He couldn't hear above his rattling quills and rushing blood, nor could he see past the clutch of feeding females.

Closer to home, a ruffed grouse drums behind the house, the sound like a Ping-Pong ball losing its bounce. I stalk the bird, but it senses me or some other danger and lapses into silence before I can find him. I can picture how he looked, however, with his stiff ruff, his spread tail, his wings cupping air in great claps of sound.

Desire is everywhere, shaping what we see as much as what we feel, but it's desire of a different kind that occupies me today, prompted by an on-air discussion of the push to restore southern red wolves to their former habitat.

The concept is fraught with dilemmas. For starters, the agency behind the restoration program, the U.S. Fish and Wildlife Service, is the same branch of government that once worked to exterminate all wolves from the country, riding a wave of hate that included some of the nation's leading conservationists. John Burroughs thought predators like wolves "certainly need killing." Theodore Roosevelt called them beasts "of waste and desolation." And William Hornaday, an early leader of the wildlife conservation movement and author of *The American Natural History*, found them "despicable. There is no depth of meanness, treachery, or cruelty to which [wolves] do not cheerfully descend."

One hundred years later, the mood has clearly changed, desire providing a wholly different lens through which to view this animal. The southern red wolf, *Canis rufus*, is described as smaller than the gray wolf and sturdier and redder than most coyotes. Its original territory is believed to have included the whole Southeast, but it didn't have the survival tactics to endure both habitat destruction and massive eradication efforts, and it was declared extinct in the wild in 1980. The coyote's arrival may have been the final straw, however, as the last wild wolves had begun interbreeding with coyotes, thus diluting and further dissipating the original genetic stock. It's that singular act that biologists want to stop — a sexual misunion speeding up the erasure of a once distinct species.

Seen another way, however, mating with coyotes may simply have been the wolf's last option for keeping itself alive. Coyotes were available; wolf partners were not. And in that instinctive drive to perpetuate the species, the red wolf availed itself of the next best solution and produced a litter of hybrids with traits from both parents.

That same survival tactic worked for the remaining gray wolves in Canada, at least the way I imagine it, the gray wolf and the coyote finding each other on a cold February day in Ontario. But the very fact that they could do so raises difficult questions about our notion of "species." The definition most of us grew up with (now called the "Biological Species Concept") defines a species as a group of organisms able to produce fertile offspring only with organisms like themselves. The classic case in point is that of mating a horse with a donkey — it's possible to do so, but the offspring is the infertile mule, which is not a viable species. The definition is supported by the same logic Darwin presented in *The Origin of Species*, when he concluded that the offspring of species that interbreed would be sterile, "for species within the same country could hardly have kept distinct had they been capable of crossing freely."

Since Darwin's time, however, we've learned that hybridization is common among plants and may have taken place in birds far more often than was originally believed. Since plants are stationary, they have to rely, both for pollination and for seed dispersal, on whatever might arrive on the wind or on the wings and legs of insects and birds. They couldn't have developed such an array of color, scent, and shape if they hadn't been receptive to cross-pollination. Birds, as it turns out, also interbreed, which seems hard to believe, given the frequency of exact replicas, generation after generation looking just like their parents. Yet a walk around a city pond reveals just how often ducks interbreed — mallards, in particular, seem quite willing to mate with Muscovys, with black ducks, even with the elegant pintails, producing ragged-looking, patched-together combinations. Such unions happen far from urban centers as well. Current estimates suggest that 10 percent of the ten thousand species of birds in the world have been known to interbreed and produce hybrid offspring (such as the offspring produced when golden-winged and blue-winged warblers mate, called either a Lawrence's warbler or a Brewster's warbler, depending on the resulting coloration).

Hybridization among mammals, however, continues to be rare, which makes the unions of wolves and coyotes even more intriguing. Though it may seem surprising that mammals in proximity don't freely cross, that's probably a very human attitude toward primitive behaviors. Our ideas about sexual appetites tend to have little to do with the practices of wild animals, as when we call a man obsessed with sex a "wolf," despite the fact that a wolf adheres to strict social taboos, is incredibly fastidious about its choice of mate, and has a very short season to act on its sexual desires, which arise at the bitterest time of year.

The isolating mechanisms that keep similar species distinct can still be explained by what Darwin called "kinship competition" and the "principle of divergence." According to the first theory, similarly designed animals (kin) would be at each other's throats if they vied for the same food and den sites. In order to avoid such a competitive, calorie-consuming existence, they diverged, becoming specialized in slightly different areas. Among the large canine predators, wolves evolved a heartier build and more powerful jaws, which, though expensive to maintain, meant they were in a niche by themselves, with little competition for the large prey they fed on (caribou, elk, moose, deer); meanwhile, coyotes evolved a less limited palate and stomachs that could tolerate almost anything.

What we may also be seeing in these unions, however, is another function of divergence that is far more difficult to study. Seen through the lens of mutualism, it may be vitally important for similar species to live close enough that they might help sustain each other in times of habitat disasters. Should a species be exposed to great duress, it might benefit from an infusion of genetic material from nearby close relatives, a supplement that might make the difference between dying and living. Coyotes and wolves, similar and yet different, appear to have done just that, tapping each other's gene pools to cope with eradication efforts. They hybridized — producing fertile offspring — and augmented each other's genetic resources, a move of particular benefit to the coyote. For the wolf, the infusion may have staved off extinction, though it may also have further diminished the stock of genetically pure wolves.

In a broader sense, mutualism also helps explain the appeal of biodiversity for a very simple reason: the greater the number of distinct gene pools in the world, the greater the chances of keeping everybody healthy, as such abundance keeps alive the possibility of gene infusions from nearby kin. A push in the opposite direction, toward monoculture, is the antithesis of this concept of health. The elimination of species diversity, which we're witnessing in the production of most fruits and vegetables, is a setup for environmental disaster. Plants designed for uniformity, grown in total isolation from any close kin, lose their ability to protect themselves against fast-evolving insects and disease; their existence can be maintained only by chemists and plant pathologists (or by labor-intensive gardeners like me, who will squash as many bean beetle larvae as I can tolerate until the season is almost over and it's possible to ignore the last of the shredded leaves and pocked beans).

Mutualism may also be the best explanation for the red wolf–eastern coyote entanglements, though few in the U.S. Fish and Wildlife Service want to believe that possibility. With large cash

infusions available through the Endangered Species Act, the
agency has initiated a captive breeding program to try to maintain a pure stock of the remaining red wolves. Over a period of
six years, they trapped more than four hundred wild canids in the
last remnant of red wolf territory in southwestern Louisiana and
southeastern Texas, all of which bore a physical resemblance to a
red wolf. They then did genetic testing on the animals, with dis-
appointing results. According to their published description of
the project, only forty-three of the original four hundred animals
were considered true red wolves, a number reduced to fourteen
after subsequent breeding experiments.

The resulting offspring seemed genetically pure and were al-
lowed to continue breeding, with a target goal of 330 animals in
captivity. (At the time of this writing, they are two-thirds of the
way there, with captive wolves being raised at thirty-three facili-
ties nationwide.) The success of the breeding program has created
another dilemma for the Fish and Wildlife Service — where to re-
locate at least 220 animals. Public hatred of wolves doomed at
least one possible site, and the sheer density of coyotes ruined another, as the newly released wolves found coyote partners for
mates, forcing biologists to find and destroy all of the hybrid litters. At present, however, there has been at least one success, with
several dozen wild red wolves holding their own in the Alligator
River National Wildlife Refuge in North Carolina.

But whether or not these are true red wolves is hotly debated,
a taxonomic conundrum that still shadows the eastern coyote.
Species identification in the coyote-wolf world requires far more
information than whether the offspring are fertile or not. Scientists have to rely on a series of comparisons, including the results of genetic testing, the sizes of skulls and teeth, and such behaviors as methods of hunting, choice of prey, and rates of social
acceptance among nonpack or family members. The first of these,
the DNA tests, suggested that the southern red wolf was, in fact,

intermediary between coyotes and gray wolves. But because this could have been caused by red wolves and coyotes slipping off together far earlier than was initially suspected, scientists had to find DNA from specimens untainted by such matings. They found a source in the Smithsonian Institution's fur vault, which contains the nation's purest collection of red wolf pelts, gathered from wild wolves in the early 1900s. However, no distinct red wolf genotype was found in these samples, at least not with the particular test they were using — that of mitochondrial DNA (mtDNA).

The one catch of this test is that mtDNA, which is different from the DNA found in the nucleus of cells, is a cloned replica of the mother's genetic makeup; it doesn't contain any of the father's DNA. (Such tests did offer additional proof that wolf-coyote unions happen only one way — with wolf fathers and coyote mothers, probably because a female wolf would never tolerate the advances of the smaller male coyote.) Researchers then turned to nuclear DNA testing, a more sophisticated process that isn't dependent on the sex of the parent. Here again, however, they came up with the same results. They found no specific red wolf genetic markers, either in the existing populations or in those long dead and held in the Smithsonian's vault. The current conclusion, according to Robert Wayne, a molecular geneticist from UCLA, is that the red wolf "may have been a subspecies similar to the Mexican [gray] wolf," and that both subspecies are smaller than the gray wolf, *Canis lupus*. In as modulated a tone as seems possible for such a contentious issue, Wayne concedes that fossil evidence may suggest that "present-day red wolves are descendants of a now extinct unique southern subspecies of gray wolf," but they can no longer be distinguished as a separate species today. Researchers such as Ron Nowak, of the U.S. Fish and Wildlife Service, completely disagree, claiming that skull measurements prove the existence of two different wolf species alive today — *Canis lupus* and *Canis rufus* — and that measuring skulls is a far better test than that of DNA, which depends on a finite library of genetic possibilities.

Settling the controversy may require more sophisticated DNA analyses or more finely tuned studies of the behaviors and ecology of these respective populations, but in the meantime, Robert Wayne offers an explanation for that odd and influential moment when coyotes and gray wolves mated somewhere in southern Ontario. It's not an event that could happen again, he says. Since the Endangered Species Act was passed in 1973, he writes, gray wolves "are once more flourishing in Minnesota . . . [H]ybridization with coyotes is no longer occurring, and gray wolves have been observed actively to exclude coyotes from their territories. Therefore not only did hybridization happen under unnatural conditions, it does not persist when the causal factors are reversed."

Yet such is not the case with another small population of wolves under considerable duress — the Algonquin wolves of eastern Ontario, so named for the provincial park they inhabit (an increasingly popular place for visitors who come for the chance that wolves will respond to their howls). The husband-and-wife team of John and Mary Theberge used radio collars to follow wolves for eleven uninterrupted years, tracking them from both the ground and the air. In the last few years of their work, they began noticing smallish wolves with a few unwolf-like behaviors. The wolves, they guessed, had begun hybridizing with coyotes, though the majority of them hadn't yet been affected by coyote genetic material, physically or ecologically.

According to the Theberges, Algonquin wolves continue to eat large prey almost exclusively; their body weight is that of wolves, as are their territories and pack sizes, and their howls are resonant and deep, "not yippy and nasal like coyotes." Yet there are those few behavioral exceptions, such as the quick social acceptance of nonpack members, a trait typical of coyotes. And there are those animals that hunt in a split-pack fashion rather than as a whole pack, which again is more common among coyotes than wolves. The one piece of evidence that might prove to be the wolves' undoing is the number of skulls from Algonquin wolves that are statistically smaller than the average wolf's skull.

So what do the Theberges believe they've been studying? Here again the genetic tests raise more questions than answers. After eleven years of close contact with the animals, the Theberges feel they know them well, individually and collectively — their ages, their scars, their home ranges, their dens, the pitch at which they howl, and the distance they might roam in a season or a year — yet they can't state their taxonomic status without some hesitation. In 1987, when they renewed their study (piggybacking on research they had conducted in the sixties and seventies), they weren't sure whether the animals were an isolated population of red wolves, a unique and undefined species of wolf (neither red nor gray), or a distinct subspecies of the gray wolf. Ten years later, with the threat of coyote gene-swamping looming larger, they conducted genetic tests on blood samples taken from their radio-collared subjects.

The results confirmed that hybridization with coyotes had occurred in at least 16 percent of their samples. Yet more surprising was the apparent proof that the Algonquin and southern red wolves are genetically identical. Each is a remnant population of a species that once occupied a far larger range, and each is at risk of irreversible dilution of its gene pool. Buoyed by these findings, the Theberges have proposed that the two species be reclassified as one, *Canis lycaon*, a move that would bolster protection for the wolves both within and outside of Algonquin Provincial Park, "the last refuge of the purest remaining lycaon wolf."

Canada doesn't yet have an Endangered Species Act, but the red wolf's designation as pure wolf in the United States could help secure its protection in the provinces to the north. Currently, the

Algonquin wolves can be shot or snared whenever they leave the park, which happens each winter when they follow the deer herds toward the outlying farms. The Theberges have witnessed mortality rates as high as 61 percent, with most wolves killed not by commercial trappers but by "people who don't like them" and who readily destroy the identifying collars. Such high death rates can disrupt the pack's social fabric, as when a line of snares wipes out most of a family (the other members tend to linger, unable to help, as one and then another are caught with wire loops around their necks). Wolves on their own, without the controls of a family network, turn to nearby coyotes or coyote-wolf hybrids for mates. It's a pattern that no one is certain can be reversed. The U.S. Fish and Wildlife Service freely admits that it doesn't know whether the red wolf will be able to maintain "its genetic integrity in the presence of a coyote population, assuming otherwise favorable circumstances . . . The final answer can only be determined by actual trial."

Meanwhile, a seventy-two-pound, coyotelike animal has been shot in Glover, Vermont, and no one knows exactly what it is, as it's fifteen pounds heftier than the biggest male coyotes. Blood samples are taken, a lab is consulted, but genetic results haven't provided any conclusions.

"We like to think that DNA is definite," says Kimberly Royar of Vermont's Department of Fish and Wildlife, "and yet we get back contradictory information from the labs. We can send DNA samples from the same animal to two different labs and be told two different things." Or three different things, as in the case of the Glover canid. Preliminary DNA findings suggest that it was an Algonquin wolf, that it was a coyote, and that it was a mix of wolf, coyote, and Siberian husky.

The small town of Glover, in northern Vermont, is not that far from southern Ontario, and from there it's only a few hours' drive into the heart of Algonquin Park, where wolves continue to do such uncoyote-like things as killing moose, forming tight packs, and howling from so deep in their chests that no one could mistake them for thin-voiced coyotes. Unfortunately, no one confirmed the wail of the Glover canid before it was shot; no one recorded its associations with other animals. The only thing state biologists know for sure is that the huge animal was killed in an area saturated by coyotes.

"Everything we thought we knew about the eastern coyote," Royar says, "has been thrown to the wind, at least in terms of its niche and genetics and interbreeding possibilities." I like the way she hits those words — *thought we knew*. I feel the same pleasure when weather systems elude forecasters, or northern lights make the full moon look shrouded in red, and no one could have predicted the show. "Ten to fifteen years ago," she says, "I collected a number of reports of large canids, but at the time I wasn't thinking that they were anything but coyotes, and I didn't take photographs or DNA samples. Now I wish I had, because of what we're learning about the coyote-wolf hybrids. It seems as though the coyote has foiled our expectations once again."

Her colleague John Hall sounds similarly curious and bemused. "The animals are continuing to evolve to fit New England's changing habitats," he says. But that's where the definitive claims seem to end. "What will be fascinating to see, twenty years from now, is whether or not we'll still think of them as coyotes."

The final naming, when it does come, may have several implications. I suspect one of them may be similar to the findings of Peter and Rosemary Grant, who are studying species adaptations among Darwin's finches on the Galápagos Islands. What they've been discovering over the past twenty years, as chronicled by Jonathan Weiner in *The Beak of the Finch*, is the astonishing fact that natural selection, contrary to Darwin's notion of its centuries-slow pace, is happening every hour of every day. Though the pace of natural selection must certainly be slower in regions with hard winters, in the tropical islands of the Galápagos, sudden changes in the birds' habitat, such as a drought or a flood, can cause a furious pace of adaptations, producing slight but noticeable changes in each successive generation.

As Rosemary Grant puts it, "Species don't stand still. You can't 'preserve' a species."

Presuming her claim is as true for large mammals as it is for birds, then the red wolf has apparently done just that — refused to stand still, whether in Tennessee, North Carolina, or Ontario. Instead, it may have done what was necessary to preserve itself, albeit as a slightly different species. Uniting with the coyote may have been the protective measure that helped each advance. And though the wolf had to undergo the more dramatic of the pair's changes, the coyote's influence may mean the red wolf will be less susceptible to the changing moods of the humans quickly encroaching on its turf. As the Theberges point out, the wolf is ill adapted to coexist with humans; the coyote, on the other hand, appears to be doing just fine.

IT'S HOLLY'S BIRTHDAY, and we linger over breakfast, assessing some of the bigger changes we have seen these past few years — births, deaths, new jobs, new friends, a hip that she can trust again and a world that seems larger as a consequence. Her only lingering sadness is that her kids live so far away, but they will soon be calling to help bridge the distance on this day, and I have to get ready for another day at school.

That's when I see a red fox cross the road just south of the house, its head high with something held in its mouth, which looks like a grouse given its color and size. The fox follows the brook and doesn't swerve from what's clearly a direct path to the den on the hill.

Disappointment rushes through me; I was holding out hope that the den might be a coyote's. And then, of course, the litheness of the animal erases that feeling. It's burnished and gorgeous and fluid, and I recall one of Thoreau's many descriptions of a fox. "He runs as though there were not a bone in his back," he writes, as part of an homage in "A Natural History of Massachusetts." "When I see a fox run across the pond on the snow with the carelessness of freedom, or at intervals trace his course in the sunshine along the ridge of a hill, I give up to him sun and earth as to their true proprietor."

I, too, give him his due and then have to hurry to get to class on time.

17

THE FAST-GROWING KITTEN can't bear living inside any longer. She has had all her shots, she's been spayed, the stitches pulled, and at last I open the door and let her explore the world outside. She sniffs, she rolls, she hightails it across the grass, a curious sideways leaping, as though testing the seam where her shadow attaches. I take a book along into the spring sun, sure she'll play for hours within sight of the house, until I look up from the page and realize she's gone.

"Stella," I yell. "Stella." I wince with guilt, wondering if in some perverse way I wanted this, a test of a coyote's presence, using a cat for bait. I can hear the voice of the forester who, when I asked him what he thought had changed since coyotes entered the area, said, "Only that no one keeps cats anymore."

Fortunately, that guilty thought fades fast; I'm already too fond of her, even when she walks on my pillow at night or gets my attention by tugging her claws through the one upholstered chair.

"Stella," I yell again. Then I see her in the field, an orange-gray streak, bounding toward me with something in her mouth.

A ruffed grouse chick.

I'm too stunned to move. I can't believe she's captured prey already. I can't believe she heard the bevy of baby birds across the field at the edge of the woods. I had no idea they were nesting so close, or that their eggs could have hatched already. I had seen two adult birds earlier in the winter, sometime after the first snow fell, as they stretched on tiptoe into the barberry bushes, cleaning out all the red fruit. And I'd heard the drumming of a male grouse in the spring. But I hadn't expected this — a clutch of nearby chicks, mottled tan and black, and a cat almost the same color, instinct-driven and very, very fast.

IN THE GARDEN, I stoop to inspect the first planting of lettuce — a mix of oak leaf and romaine, reds and greens, all of it about a quarter-inch high — and look up to see two of last summer's fawns, not thirty feet away.

They show no great fear of me, though at least they go through some of the motions; they bound, tails half cocked, toward the brook. There they linger, resisting the urge to twitch or shift, as we observe each other through the leafless trees.

I think of the resignation I heard in the voice of an orchardist, whose family has supplied the area with apples for three generations, when he talked about the current plague of deer. "There's way too many of them," he said. "I might see a herd of twenty to thirty, in the middle of the day, feeding on the trees. They're fearless, now that fewer hunters take to the woods each year. More coyotes would help, but they're what's getting shot."

I wonder where the coyotes are. Though I have found evidence of them farther back in the woods, I have seen no sign of them on our land in too many months. I'm not even sure I've heard them since the night after we moved in, though they have howled several times in my dreams. Perhaps I've cleaned out too many of the necessary edges, cutting back the undergrowth around the pines and along the old field, making it easier to see through the woods. Perhaps they sense my scrutiny, my desire to have them close; such intense attention has never served them well. Or perhaps they were here only for the brief abandonment, the months after the last owners quit the house and barn and let the lawns and field grow deep in weeds and grasses. Then we came, removed the best cover, and, after two seasons, stopped tossing dead mice.

It's deer that find this place increasingly attractive.

The familiar conflict rushes in: I love seeing them here, and I hate having them so close. Again, I wish for more coyotes. And again I hear all the reasons we should fear the latter's impact — stories overheard at school or in restaurants, in town or in letters to the editors, all decrying the ruthless tactics of this rapacious predator. Deer hunters complain about coming home empty-handed when they hunt the nearby hills, despite their skill, despite having hunted these woods for years. It's obvious, they insist, that coyotes are responsible. By killing the fawns, coyotes are decimating next year's herd. By taking mature deer, they're wiping out future breeders.

What I don't seem to find in these high-pitched portrayals are reasons that the overall deer population is currently at a record level in the Northeast, easily outpacing the number of hunters. It's too easy to blame the competition when a hunter is unsuccessful, the way seals are accused of pinching fishermen's yields, or foxes are faulted for their preference for pheasant. It's true that coyotes eat calves and lambs, and that fawn hooves show up now and again in coyote scat. It's also true that deer carcasses can be found in the woods, with that unmistakable rear-end entry of the coyote. But it can less often be proved that coyotes did the actual killing, that it wasn't injury or disease that weakened the deer first and left it unable to survive the extremes of hunger and ice.

What the anti-coyote people definitely don't want to hear are the findings of two recent studies of the mortality rates of fawns. In the first, a research team in Massachusetts spent months radio-tracking herds in various parts of the state and discovered that young deer are falling prey to two different predators, each group taking almost equal numbers of the fawns: coyotes and poachers — those hunters who can't wait until the season legally opens. In the second study, researchers in Pennsylvania also radio-collared fawns and found that bears and coyotes killed almost equal numbers of fawns, though mortality due to natural causes accounted for twice as many deaths as those caused by predators.

I watch these deer watch me, with their large dark eyes and

graceful limbs, and I want to stay held in this moment, to think of them as "the untainted manifestation of the Divine." And then I want to shout them away. Their large bodies represent what's hardest about the edges where we all meet — coyotes, deer, skunks, raccoons, potato bugs, me. I seem to be clear only in my dealings with the smallest, and then only when they enter the house or the garden. Mice show up in our drawers, and I trap them. Potato bugs hump across green leaves — or cucumber beetles or cabbage moth caterpillars — and I don't hesitate to destroy them. But a deer? I'll tie pie tins to slender apple trees and endure their banging in the breeze. I'll set out a transistor radio in a plastic bag, tuned to a talk show that plays through the night. I'll wrap up small satchels of Holly's or my hair and pin them to posts at the garden's corners. I'll even line the perimeter with a stream of my own pee before I'll call in a hunter to shoot them. I'll also stop a neighbor's dog from running down a deer, and cheer if a coyote does the same thing.

Yet the situation I saw on offshore islands, when I traveled by boat from my home on Deer Isle, suggests we have few alternatives when faced with too many deer. The island herds had wiped out most of the available food, and even feeding on landscaped plantings and on the hay left by concerned citizens couldn't avert slow starvation. There is no island predator that can keep them in check. The same dilemma exists inland, where the increased number of suburban deer has meant more collisions with cars, more entanglements with dogs, and more sustained damage to crops and orchards.

I say, Bring on the coyotes. But don't make them feel too welcome. And don't leave out food for them — no mouse bodies, no young cats left out overnight — or the experiment will backfire, and they'll settle into the easier life, feeding off us instead.

HAD I MORE TIME, I could probably learn to distinguish between the different deer in the field, the one that likes chard, for example, from the one that seems to prefer the tips of saplings growing by the brook. Figuring out their individual features shouldn't be that complicated (I have, after all, learned the names of more than one hundred students by the second week of a semester), and their home ranges aren't that large — only about one square mile of land for three seasons of the year. But if I knew each one by sight, my affections would become more complicated, as would my ability to race at them, yelling.

With coyotes, it is different. Not only are they more elusive than deer, but their home ranges can extend from two to thirty square miles, depending on who's doing the estimating. In Jonathan Way's studies of the suburban coyotes of Cape Cod, radio-collared animals were found to occupy ranges between six and eighteen square miles, using such natural and man-made boundaries as highways and rivers, lakes and the ocean. The coyote with the smallest range lived in one of the most densely populated areas of the Cape (a finding that intimates much about the ease of suburban living), while one unmated male covered an area of about fifty square miles. On any given night, a coyote might travel about ten miles, which, in most areas, means crossing backyards in a lot of different neighborhoods.

Jon Way's studies have also confirmed the findings of other researchers — dispersing coyotes will move into an empty territory within days or weeks after the previous occupant has died or experienced some disruption. "It's fruitless," he says, "to kill coyotes in a specific area simply to get rid of the coyotes." The space left behind is simply a space to be filled, with another coyote quickly taking its place.

This tendency to travel seems innate in coyote behavior. It's that fact, along with a remarkable endocrine system, that accounts for their unprecedented numbers and their ability to survive every effort to eradicate them. For not only are coyotes designed to find unoccupied home ranges, their response to undue pressures

— bounties, M-44 chargers, Compound 1080, or coyote derbies — is to have larger litters, an unusual practice among birds and animals.

Most species, when food is scarce, will give birth to fewer young or, like the wood stork, refrain from nesting altogether. Both responses occur among wolves, which either tailor the size of their litters to available game or don't breed at all in a hard year. (If persecution becomes too intense, however, the social structure of wolves may break down, and all female wolves may produce litters, or the solo male wolves may locate unmated coyotes.) Coyotes, on the other hand, aren't confined by such rigid social organization. For them the overriding imperative is staying alive, and somehow their reproductive systems know to kick in when life's trials become most arduous. The result can be litters of up to twelve pups, a staggeringly large number in difficult times, adding more young to the number of coyotes looking for available space to call home, somewhere between Alaska and the Panama Canal.

When the three-year-old boy was attacked on Cape Cod, it was the first life-threatening coyote assault recorded in New England. But at least fifty other coyote attacks have occurred in five other states and a few provinces in Canada, though so far with only one known fatality — that of another three-year-old child, killed by coyotes in Los Angeles. The vulnerability of small children is very real, however, as detailed in a report by the Canadian Wildlife Service and summarized by Gerry Parker in *Eastern Coyote*. These victims range from the toddler a coyote grabbed in Yellowstone National Park (the child was bruised and required twenty-one stitches to patch up her face, "but was generally protected by a heavy snowsuit") to the two-year-old girl a coyote carried off from a backyard near Jasper National Park ("the coyote's jaws appeared to be clamped around the throat and neck of the child [though it] dropped the child as her parents rushed toward it. The unconscious child was rushed to a nearby hospital with extensive injuries around the face, neck, and throat. However, the child recovered"). That a coyote would look at a small child and see a tidy parcel of food makes sense, especially if that coyote had learned to associate humans with handouts. Yet the coyotes may also be showing us how best to keep them at bay.

We know they respect territory — they're quick to mark newly claimed land with urine and scent glands and carefully deposited scat; they also announce their claim with a range of different howls. What we haven't yet learned is how to mark our own territory in a way they will regard as equally effective. William Davis, who works for MassWildlife, recommends that people be both assertive and aggressive. If a coyote is making itself obvious in some way, if it's no longer attempting to stay hidden, then take every opportunity to scare it off, Davis says, using loud noises, bright lights, even the beam reflected from a mirror. "We encourage adults to walk toward the animal slowly but deliberately," he says. "Throw tennis balls, whatever is handy. When you get to the edge of your property line, that's where you stop. They'll know that's your territory."

It's something I've been doing halfheartedly with deer, though my inconsistency must present a mixed message at best. But with coyotes, I'm aiming for a clearer relationship, no longer handing out dead mice or scraps of food, the way I did with that fox on Deer Isle. I was never quite sure I hadn't led indirectly to the fox's demise, as I didn't see it again until I read *Wild Fox*, a children's book by our neighbor Cherie Mason about the three-legged fox that appeared in her yard the next winter, cautious on its new stump and keen to eat the seeds from her bird feeders.

Other people in this area are feeding foxes; I've heard their stories. They're also feeding bears and deer, despite the fact that it's illegal (though it's not against the law for the local farm and garden supply store to sell specially packaged deer food). This takes commensal relationships a little too far, inviting animals to eat with us, expecting them to know friend from foe. Some animals can learn to make that distinction, as in a story Jon Way tells about a coyote that liked to sun atop a rock at a golf course, ignoring the people regularly passing by until it saw Jon, started barking, and kept it up for a solid fifteen minutes. The maintenance crew couldn't figure out what he had done to alarm it, but the animal's reaction, Jon surmised, was probably due to his relentless pursuit of them, often through the night with his truck and flashlight and radio receiver. Most wild animals, however, who have had too much easy contact with us — too many doughnuts or chicken bones or easy piles of deer corn — will eventually be surprised, not by a handout, but by the click of a gun's safety release.

In addition to Davis's tactics to define our respective limits, we may also want to imitate more specific message-signaling. Coyotes can convey all kinds of messages — time to rest, time to play, time to eat, time to surrender — using a complex system of face, tail, ear, and hackle displays (though it's still not quite clear exactly how they convey the hardlearned lesson *Don't eat that stuff*). They also employ such vocalizations as growls, huffs, barks, whines, yelps, and howls (with the group "yip-howl" producing what one researcher has likened to "screams, gargles and laughs"). With a little training, perhaps we, too, could manage a stay-away, don't-mess-with-me growl. It may even become one of those job skills that show up on an animal control officer's résumé: "Able to give the alpha male message. Able to signal, All clear."

First, however, we have to improve our skills at listening.

Kathy O'Rourke, a naturalist who lives in Shelburne Falls, tells a story about coyotes and listening, from the winter she spent as a ranger at Chaco Canyon in New Mexico. She had become fond of one particular coyote, an animal she passed often as she bicycled to and from work and whom she looked forward to seeing every day. Then he was shot. She heard the gunfire, she followed the tracks and sat with him while he died.

The following day, after the questions and jokes and necessary paperwork with the park police, she learned from Tucsohn, a Navajo coworker, that the shooter had been a young Navajo man. She hadn't asked Tucsohn the question; he had simply sensed her need to know why it had happened. "The People think it is bad luck when a coyote crosses your path," he told her. "Harm may come to you. So you have to break the coyote's spirit, kill him or sprinkle corn pollen on his tracks." He had his own pouch of protective pollen, but others opted for more dramatic responses, particularly those who no longer followed the old ways, and the young gunner might have been one of them. Tucsohn then explained that a Navajo had recently been bitten — "That hasn't happened before," she quotes him as saying — and the animal was shot in retaliation.

According to Tucsohn, however, the bite was about more than a few puncture wounds; the coyote wanted to convey a message. "Coyote was trying to warn the People about the asbestos plant," he said, a potentially toxic project scheduled to be built on reservation land.

18

ACCORDING TO MANY local residents — particularly the hunters who might each kill a dozen coyotes every winter — the animal is an invasive, an alien with no right to be here. Technically, however, "invasive" refers to a species whose arrival disrupts or displaces those that already occupy the land, and coyotes haven't displaced anything. The niche they now inhabit was wide-open when they arrived, unused for almost one hundred years. As for any disruption they may have caused — that remains to be seen. There's still too much shifting and accommodating to know for sure.

Several studies have suggested that their presence is hard on foxes, which are said to move out when coyotes move in, but judging from the number of active dens I've seen or heard about this spring, red foxes seem to be thriving, at least in this county. Of course, they may be dealing with coyote pressures by moving closer to human activity, where a coyote might have less cover as it lies in wait for a lunch of fox kit. The impact of coyotes on the more secretive gray fox is also unclear, though the fox's ability to climb trees may help it elude the larger predator.

A more accurate example of invasive is the tiny insect that's currently poised to destroy one of the sturdiest trees in our forests. The hemlock woolly adelgid has already decimated stands of hemlock to the south of us and has recently been found just a few miles away. We'll know they're here when tiny fluffs of white wool appear on those graceful hemlock branches, or when the nymphs hatch, streaming from eggs in April or May, each trailing its own spot of wool through new needles.

Like aphids, the adelgids will start sucking sap. Unlike aphids, they have no known U.S. predators. In Japan, where they originated, a kind of mite and the ladybird beetle help keep them in check. Here the trees are defenseless, and all may be infested within the next ten years or so. So far, no spray seems to work. Fertilizing the trees in an attempt to keep them healthy serves instead to fortify the insects. And once the tree has been infested, vital sap drawn from its core, it's a slow death from the lower limbs all the way to the crown. Four years is a typical life span once adelgids have started to suck.

I will miss the trees when they're gone. Our landscape will be pocked, brooks and rivers exposed, north-facing slopes left naked. And in the nearby state forests, where stands of old growth remain, hemlocks that predate European settlement — trees that have survived wind and ice storms for over four hundred years — may soon be felled by a puny little insect.

Nothing about the coyote's story compares with that; one is about total devastation, the other about a new arrival, like a cardinal, an opossum, a noisy Carolina wren.

HOLLY IS AWAY for the weekend, the brooks on either side of the house swell with rain, and neither the cat nor I can sleep. The sound of rushing water drowns out all other noise, except the 3 A.M. train that wails at each crossing. Stella stalks along the walls; she sniffs baseboards and chair legs; she stiffens her legs and acts restless on her toes. Something must have moved through in the dark, leaving a story I'm not able to smell; or else something is outside still, exuding its raw scent, which is seeping right now through the cracks of the house.

She smacks at a wall, she follows a sound with her eyes, she leaps about in frustration. Then she freezes; she flattens; she pees on the floor.

I don't go back to bed after cleaning up the mess. Instead, I watch the sky lighten and feel the way dawn subdues the night's noises. I can't see what might have upset the kitten, but she's reluctant to go outside when I open the door.

Instead, she curls into my lap when I'm settled with a cup of coffee, her purr becoming a thrum against my legs. Soon I will have to get on my hands and knees and see what might be living under the porch. A few days ago, I noticed a new scrape and hollow, just large enough for some chunky body to squeeze under the sill. But I'm reluctant to get out a flashlight and peer around for eyes. I'd like it to be a coyote, but that's not how I want to discover the animal, while I'm on my belly in the middle of its escape route.

Stella leaps from my lap, two sets of needle prints in my legs, and I realize I can't wait any longer. I pull on pants and a jacket and make sure the flashlight works. Then I leave the kitten inside and head for the front yard. The rushing brooks make the land feel alive, as though water were seeping from every vessel and vein, every root and tuber and bulb.

I shimmy halfway under the porch and shine the light in all four corners. Nothing stares back. No yellow eyes; no red ones. No balled body that I can see. There is a strong odor, however, a recent and rank smell that isn't cat or dog.

I rub my hand on the wood around the opening, a way to mark the space with a smell that might discourage whatever spent the night from returning. But I really don't know why that would work. My smell's already all over the property, and that hasn't slowed any of the traffic in night animals.

I PAUSE AT THE EDGE of the raspberry row, and a sudden shadow passes over me, large enough to make me duck as I look for the source — a turkey vulture, one of eight riding air currents above me, a bird far larger than any I saw in my childhood. The largest land birds I saw as a kid were the occasional raven, an osprey, a red-tailed hawk. But vultures, with their six-foot wingspan, make the others look small, and I remember one of Thoreau's comments about the absence of large animals in his landscape.

"When I consider that the nobler animals have been exterminated here," he wrote in his journal in 1856, "the cougar, panther, lynx, wolverene [sic], wolf, bear, moose, deer, the beaver, the turkey, etc., etc., — I cannot but feel as if I lived in a tamed, and, as it were, emasculated country . . . Is it not a maimed and imperfect nature that I am conversant with?"

He needn't have worried about the permanence of the decline. Although it took over one hundred years, the last five species on his list have returned, five big presences we're learning how to live with in this landscape. Two others, though not returnees, bring that number to seven — the coyote, a species Thoreau couldn't have anticipated, and vultures, lured north as the interstate highways were completed, their shoulders new sources of roadkill. Both species respond in similar ways to death — they gather, whether to the remains of a poached deer or to a cow that the farmer, instead of burying, pulled behind his tractor to the edge of the woods. They also benefit in similar ways from our excess and recklessness. And each thrives despite having no history here. As with coyotes, there is no Yankee mythology about vultures, no place in native tales where the mention of a buzzard circling a field, of a line of dark birds on a roof, or of someone caught in a large shadow is sure to ratchet up a story's tension.

Another returnee of sorts, at least to the highest and northernmost parts of our region, is the raven. Its numbers dropped radically after wolves were extirpated, as ravens often survived on the remains of wolf-killed prey. (According to Linda Hogan, "It is thought that they direct the wolves to their prey, then stand by until the carcass is relinquished to them for their own earned share in the feast.") But ravens are again on the rise, though not along roadsides, which is the vulture's domain, but in the Adirondacks, the Green Mountains, the thick woods of Maine, living on meat scrounged from coyote kills.

Though all of these large animals appeared at different times over the last hundred years, that's still considerable change for any habitat to absorb. Yet those are just the most noticeable of the new transformations; more difficult to perceive are changes taking place on a far smaller scale, such as that of the insects buzzing daily into our lives.

As I walk the length of the raspberry canes, deciding how much more to prune, I remember hours spent last summer knocking Japanese beetles into a can of kerosene, the way my grandfather had us do as kids, paying us to keep his roses from being shredded as the beetles fed. What I began to notice last year, however, was that about half of the time I startled a beetle, it flew off rather than dropped. I felt I was witnessing a new response mechanism, an adaptation through natural selection that I was helping influence. I don't remember so many beetle losses forty years ago, when every floating body earned me another penny, but it's a logical response to a killer like me. Beetles with the genetic sense to fly rather than fall would have a better chance of surviving in my neighborhood; they might even pass on the impulse to future generations (though tucking in their legs and dropping has served them well for years; it continues to be difficult for predators to find them when they're playing dead between blades of grass).

What I'm witnessing with the flying beetles is just one illustration of the micropressures that buffet insects and plants and animals every day. The plants in this field — the fruit trees, the rhubarb, the horseradish, the raspberries — have had to endure dramatic pressures since I first set them out, such as the record-breaking heat that arrived after weeks of protracted cold, and a complete stop to any kind of rain. They're wilting, they're struggling, but they're doing just what they're supposed to do. So are the woodland plants and shrubs. A tender green spreads across the woods, and the ferns near the brook should be splendid this summer.

Yet it's the pace of all these changes that we're just beginning to heed, a speed, as it were, that makes the arrival of large animals seem clumsy and slow in comparison. If my grandmother, who will soon be one hundred, were to assess the world outside her window today, she'd say that little had changed save that the trees had grown older, and a greater variety of birds came to her feeders each winter. Yet, as Jonathan Weiner observes in *The Beak of the Finch*, "Species of animals and plants look constant to us, but in reality each generation is a sort of palimpsest, a canvas that is painted over and over by the hand of natural selection, each time a little differently."

The only way to see such change is through careful observation for a long period of time. A hundred years is best, but, as Weiner points out, even within a few years, scientists have been able to observe natural selection at work. While studying the very finches that first inspired Darwin, researchers in the Galápagos Islands have documented violent oscillations in the birds' environments, changes occurring at any moment and at any time of day. They have been able to observe finches adapt to climate changes with changes in beak size and feeding strategies. These adaptations aren't limited to one generation, however; they're encoded in the birds' genes, affecting every hatchling that follows them.

Such flexibility is more than just the favoring of certain adaptations over others in response to selection pressure (the stoutest-beaked birds having the advantage during droughts, for example, because they can crack open even the toughest of seeds, the ones such arid conditions couldn't kill). It's also the availability or gathering of slightly altered genes, creating a readiness to respond rapidly to moisture or temperature extremes. The finches (along with all other species) are in what Weiner refers to as a constant "jittery motion," a notion that strikes him with the same force I have felt from the coyote drama unfolding around us. The very idea that species are not static rattles all of our paradigms. The concept, Weiner writes, of "evolution in action, of evolution in the flesh, has enormous implications for our sense of reality." The overall effect is quite stunning, affecting, as he says, "our sense of power, of what we can do with life."

That such changes are happening, not just with insects and birds but with the large species as well, requires a definite realigning of our expectations of what is possible. All populations are dynamic. They're jittering, they're "poised for flight," writes Weiner. They're ready to take off in a wide range of different directions, seemingly at a moment's notice.

Such ever-present motion is as much at work in finches and Japanese beetles as it is in bittersweet and loosestrife, in bears and the eastern coyote. It's a survival mechanism that helps a species cope, not just with changes in its home range but with the habitats it finds when dispersing or expanding into new territory. In addition to the ongoing, internal changes, it's also a receptivity to the infusion of genes from a similar species at difficult moments in time and for (usually) limited duration. Such events are happening right now in the Galápagos, and scientists are watching; hybrid finches appear to be thriving in response to habitat changes, and some species may even be fusing, the new, mixed form proving more successful than either of the originals. It's another startling exception to the general understanding that interbreeding often weakens a species. In the case of small birds in relative isolation, it may also give them the necessary boost to survive unexpected duress.

The coyote is also in a state of jittery motion. It has already proven receptive to gene enhancement. It mated with its longtime enemy, the wolf, while at the same time managing to adapt on a regular basis to changes in weather and terrain, to foods and obstacles, even to the oscillating populations of fleas and ticks that prefer certain patches of skin or that specific spot for gathering moisture from an eye.

Its ability to adapt, and to do so at such speed, is ample support for the prediction found in many Native American tales. If something untoward were to happen to the rest of us, these stories suggest, the coyote "will undoubtedly be the last creature left on Earth."

19

I AM IN NO HURRY to go anywhere in particular, and the dandelions are in full bloom. On impulse, after finishing errands in town, I don't take the usual route home but detour out the Old Mohawk Trail, a narrow and winding, seldom-traveled road. At the next intersection, I turn left onto Zerah Fiske Road, then take Bardwell's Ferry Road alongside fields of brilliant yellow, past hills that look sculpted in soft reds and greens. A short distance past the bridge over the Deerfield River, I recognize the dirt road a friend recently described. Drive in a half mile or so, she had said, and you'll see an old gazebo on your right. Park and follow the trail that leads down.

I do, admiring the size of the trees, the distant sound of waterfalls, the labor that went into constructing this trail. Short lengths of creosoted beams, anchored with steel cornerposts, create a series of steps that lead down to the South River. An abandoned concrete dam marks the line between a placid stream and the violent churn of a long waterfall. Its drop through the rocky ravine must be between eighty and a hundred feet. Though the quiet of the reservoir is attractive, the raging stream pulls me farther on.

Following the path here requires care, as it's a tangle of downed limbs above an eroded slope. And then it ends and the stream flattens, a site cold and loud and relatively untraveled (though several gummy bears on the path indicate other recent visitors). A building once stood here, two walls still visible in a sure fit of flat stones, the rest swept away by the high water of earlier springs.

A curved steel cradle suggests a hydroelectric operation or perhaps an old sawmill; if it's the latter, I can scarcely imagine the industry that went into such a project. The screech of a saw blade, the constant pound of the falls, the limited hours of daylight in the ravine, all for a few thousand board feet of lumber. And that would be only part of the output of labor, for the wood would have to be floated downstream and then hauled uphill to reach any destination. This, I think, would be the ultimate test of character and tenacity, commitment and endurance. But a hundred years ago, what were the options? Farming required work that was equally difficult, and the larger mills were even louder than this hollow must have been, with a boss and a clock controlling the length of the days and the output, not the sun or the logs or the sharpness of the saw.

I feel a certain awe at all that was required to build the many mills on this region's swift streams — the grist mills, woolen mills, shingle mills, cider mills, along with mills that produced broom handles, butter paddles, rolling pins, and meat mauls, snathes and rakes, blinds and sashes, doors and fence posts and sled parts. And then I add to this the image of tenacious, hardworking Yankees scrambling down this hill, full of the loneliness and heartbreak that must have come that awful spring when nothing could contain the rising flood waters. A hard life can create a hard people, and I hear again those friends in the South describing Yankees as cold and unwelcoming, as people who ate boiled eggs and made rock gardens, who were slow to help strangers or invite newcomers into their homes.

But as I wander back up the trail into quieter air, it's fear rather than reticence that I want to understand, cultural fear and the way it shaped our lives here. My own history is certainly full of it in all the genealogical lines that various relatives have traced. Individuals and whole families uprooted from Scotland, England, Wales, setting sail for the New World, coming in through the ports at Plymouth, Boston, and Halifax, Nova Scotia, driven by fear of religious persecution, fear of starvation, fear of conscription, fear of shame, fear of failure. They arrived with few resources in a land of more fear — of witches, wolves, Indian attacks, plagues, thieves, the poor farm. Yet woven throughout the stories I've heard are also the optimistic traits, a love of adventure, a desire for change and for the chance to forge new paths.

It was fear as much as stubbornness that sent me away twenty-five years ago — fear that I couldn't be myself and love whom I wanted. And it was a readiness to confront fear that made it possible to come back. What I'll never know is whether I would have done all that wandering had I not had a reason to depart, a push as much as a pull in sending me on my way. The rest of my family stayed put, as though the tendency to move had been exhausted by the generations who managed to get us here and then wanted nothing more than to grow deep roots, build solid homes, and brace for uncertain futures.

I can't stay long, however, with thoughts of what came first or how the genes were arranged. Trillium is in blossom in the woods, the dark red variety that smells like carrion and signals, for me, the end of maple sugaring season, ever since that spring I watched several buds open beneath sap buckets I had hung. Jack-in-the-pulpit is also out, in green exuberance along the roadside, while ferns scroll open in the shade, and coltsfoot leaves have begun to appear under their already blown-out blooms.

When I reach my car, I don't want to get in and instead walk slowly up the shadowed road, grateful that no clock is defining the rest of my day. And then I see it: a large, light gray animal with a dark saddle across its shoulders. A coyote, running through the nearby field.

We stop at the same time to watch each other, a sudden freezing of all forward momentum, and I feel the arc of these last months closing, as though I had known, when I detoured out this way, that it was time for the sought-for to be seen. Though I had thought it would happen at night, not in the clear light of day, that it would be murky or already dark when I'd hear a crush of dry leaves, a brush of taut body against ferns or grass, and I'd spin, I'd see yellow eyes, I'd feel a catch in my throat and smell the rankness of her body. I thought I would be the startled one.

I want that musky odor around me now, but the distance is too great, and the wind bending the grass is taking both our scents with it. She couldn't have caught mine before she launched herself from the woods. And now she isn't sure what to do, and the fear is all hers.

She lowers her head and swings it back and forth, back and forth, and I imagine she has pups stashed nearby, the need to feed them urging her forward, the need to survive for them holding her back. A long minute passes, and I wonder whether surprise is amplifying her size, and whether, up close, she looks as worn as the fox I fed in Maine, ragged from sharing all the available calories, her teats swollen and red from the tug of hungry kits.

She bolts for the woods, the grasses close around her, and I'm alone once more, on a road surrounded by fields of bounteous yellow.

I want holly to see the river, the waterfall, the effect of acres of dandelions, and the old stone building, which, a historian has since told me, was not a mill at all but a hydroelectric station. A turbine fit in that steel cradle, and the force of falling water produced enough power for an electric rail car and the town's use as well.

We wind our way down roads shaped to follow streams, under clouds that thin fast and disappear, until we're parking the car near the top of the long descent. The crash of falling water is audible from this distance, and Holly looks at the steep trail, imagines the difficult return — I can see the indecision on her face — and then starts down a step at a time. She barely pauses at the dam. She, too, wants to go farther, and we descend to the old power station.

She swings her leg gingerly, using hemlock roots to steady her balance, drawn on by the coolness, the industry, the thunder. At least, that's what I imagine. It's too loud for much talking, and for a while we sprawl on a large boulder, one of the few places in today's sudden heat where it's cool. Across the water, the blossoms of red-and-yellow columbine emerge from a slit in the rock, shadow-dappled and damp from the spray off the falls.

Though none of us can ever know how someone else takes in an experience, no matter how close we think we are to that person, I'm particularly aware of how differently Holly and I read our surroundings. Her senses are so networked that water on her skin might bring a color to mind, a fabric, a song. Or she'll feel a splash and see paisley, or skirt styles from the fifties, or the image of an apothecary's jar, her pharmacist father decanting its contents. She's a synesthete, or so I suspect from the description I found in Diane Ackerman's *Natural History of the Senses*. It's a sensory arrangement seen in the composers Scriabin and Rimski-Korsakov, both of whom associated colors with musical notes. The writer Samuel Johnson had it as well, seeing scarlet, for example, when he heard a clanging trumpet, and so did Arthur Rimbaud, who linked colors with vowel sounds. Holly's senses are as entwined as the roots and vines we just climbed through, and myriad synapses seem to be firing right now. Watching her, I feel how much stronger we are for all we have weathered, and how much freer now to wander where our respective interests take us.

I head for a downstream pool. Raccoon tracks pattern the edge, while gold pollen from birch catkins colors the ripples and eddies. It's good that we know our worlds in such different ways, and I hear again John Burroughs's grand observation: "Knowledge is only half the task. The other half is love."

THE CLIMB OUT IS SLOW, but I'd far rather have her with me today than ascend this slope alone. I hear a black-throated blue warbler and, from deeper in the woods, the flute-like songs of a pair of wood thrushes calling back and forth. Somewhere high above us, behind a screen of leaves, a scarlet tanager announces its arrival. Its journey, from Costa Rica to Conway, Massachusetts, is over for now. For a brief four months, it can stay in one small place a few square miles in size. Then it'll be gone again, the majority of its life spent elsewhere, while we stay behind and sort out the changes, wishing that blackflies didn't come with spring and that summer lasted far longer.

Back in the car, we head slowly up the narrow dirt road. I'm about to say, "There, that's where I saw it." But I don't need to.

In the same place, with the same hesitation, the coyote stops in midstride. I'm sure it must be the same animal. Holly puts her hand on my arm as we watch and wait. This time it stays longer before slipping back into the woods.

Neither of us says a thing. It's enough that a month after the last snow, with spring rushing through like a high-speed train, a coyote has appeared before us, an animal pausing in its forward run to look us over before disappearing from sight.

EVEN THOUGH I'm still keen to see a coyote on our own land, knowing one is in the vicinity has me heading toward the South River yet again. I want to find its den. And I want to be near the water, which pulls me as strongly as the Green River did when I was a child. The Green was a short walk through the woods behind our house, and it was always rife with life and possible danger. I hiked it, swam it, floated down it on inner tubes and rubber rafts. I watched muskrat and beavers there, caught dace and trout, leaves and snags, and once a hank of my best friend Karen's hair. In winter, I skated over its black ice as turtles swam underneath, and one summer, when gathering clay from a bank, I lost a tiny gold ring that had belonged to my grandmother. A year later I lost her watch when the raft I was on flipped over, an elegant watch lent me by my mother, who thought it would help me get home in time for supper. In high school, I walked all along the Green on those spring days when I could think of no other cure for my despair save watching the river slide by.

I want to find a place like that today, because school is done for the summer, a coyote is near, and I'm not ready to tackle any more projects at home. I've already torn out the old perennial beds, most of the plants choked into bloomlessness by loosestrife and mint, and I've planted as many vegetables as I dare in the garden. I'm reluctant to take on the next plumbing repair, which will have to happen soon, because the last one took several days, and instead of the easy task of replacing faucet stems, I had to replace the entire unit. And to do that, I had to pull out the whole sink, as the old bolts were rusted in place. This next project — stopping the cold drip in the showerhead upstairs — could take even longer, though I want it finished before the pending visit of an old friend.

With this particular person, nothing is ever easy, which in itself is another reason to head for the river. She was a man when we first met, married and the father of two children. Yet even then she knew she was a woman trapped inside a man's body, and she desperately wanted the experience that was genetically hers. After years of struggle and indecision, she made the break at last from one name and set of pronouns to a new wardrobe and range of possibilities. Now she is divorced, anatomically female, and more relaxed in the body she inhabits.

Though each visit makes this a little easier, I still struggle to see her for herself: a tall, odd woman with hormone-induced breasts and hips, and a voice she must work to hold high in her throat. She will stand out from the crowd no matter where she is, never quite fitting into the mainstream but always occupying an edge.

Readying the house for her visit — making sure there's reliable hot water and plenty of shelf and counter space for the new accouterments of her life — will have to wait. I can't bear to be inside, let alone cloistered in a small bathroom, and I know too well that spending hours with old plumbing will complicate my understanding of what a formerly male woman wants.

I go to the river because I'm still astounded by the speed of all these changes, and because there's nothing simple about dealing with in-betweens, whether it's a person socialized to be male who now presents herself as female, or a coyote that may be more wolf than formerly believed.

I SCRAMBLE DOWN to the dam and this time turn upstream along a trail that takes me into a dense tangle of blackberries. Impatient with the thorns and snags, I abandon the path and climb higher, where the woods are more open and lined with deer runs. On the slope, I find sagging strands of old barbed wire, an overgrown logging road, and lots of small sassafras trees. I try to imagine what this hillside looked like a hundred years ago, when all this land was open, and different species occupied it. Meadowlarks and bluebirds were the common birds then, and muskrat and woodchucks the largest of the animals.

The coyote could scarcely have survived if it tried to move in during the 1800s, when hiding places were far fewer and denning sites more vulnerable. Its diet would also have been much more limited — cherries and apples, small rodents and rabbits, and whatever young livestock it dared hunt when so many farmers were quick to grab rifles. Today its options are like those at a cafeteria, from hamburgers and French fries left at fast-food dumpsters to slow cats and lap dogs napping in backyards, from long rows of ripe melons and orchard-laden fruit to the fawns that have proliferated since open land was abandoned.

In more remote areas, the pickings are somewhat slimmer, though depending on the region, a coyote's diet might vary from a summertime mix of insects and fruit and small mammals to a winter reliance on grouse and hare and winter-starved animals, or the

remains left by hunters after every deer season. But this, too, is changing, according to Robert Chambers, a professor at SUNY's College of Environmental Science and Forestry who has studied coyotes for over thirty years. He and his students have found that in the Adirondacks, deer have become a staple for coyotes, making up 80 to 90 percent of their winter diet, while fawns make up about half of their spring and summer fare. The same coyotes also feed heavily on beavers — as much as 40 percent of their diet in the warmer seasons. It's a marked shift, Chambers points out, this killing of larger and larger prey, a behavior he describes as more like a wolf's than a coyote's.

Wolf DNA has undoubtedly played a part in these new food preferences, but Chambers also believes that the deep snow and intense cold of this rugged terrain have helped shape a better-suited coyote than the one that roams the Southwest. In the ranges of northern New York and southern Ontario, natural selection would favor strong-jawed, thick-necked animals that could kill good-sized, calorie-rich prey (an adult beaver weighs between thirty and sixty pounds, while a doe averages between eighty and a hundred pounds, though they can easily reach two hundred or more). These larger coyotes have proven to have adapted quite tidily, though what's critical to note is that it's not over yet.

"It may be most appropriate," Chambers writes, "to view the eastern coyote as a species in the process of evolution." It's still adapting, right now, as we sleep and eat and wander riverside paths.

A FURIOUS ROBIN startles me from my thoughts. I'm a few feet from the wobble of naked heads in a nest, all yellow bills and open mouths, and parents that need me gone before the feeding can resume. I hurry past and alarm a merganser, whose cries and splashing seem louder because of the string of airy ducklings struggling to keep up. They round a bend and drop out of sight, and it becomes quite clear that I am a loud visitor here, a clumsy cataloguer in a relatively untraveled place, leaving a swath as wide as a raccoon's in the raspberries.

I stay on for the silence that settles in as soon as I stop, for the sight of a gnatcatcher in a sycamore and a sapsucker just beyond, for the soft whistle of a brown creeper in a pocket of bark. A set of mink tracks follows the bank, with a scatter of crayfish claws in the water below. From here I can see where several deer, large and small, walked out onto the sand bar — to escape a swarm of blackflies, perhaps, as the breeze is stronger right above the water. But I'd like to think they did it for the view of the dark river, the soft lap of water, the feel of cool sand under their hooves. The steep bank opposite could offer some protection, as nothing could cross it quietly. Yet it could also present a difficult climb for an animal desperate to get away from either of its two predators — a coyote or a human like me.

I stay until the birds have forgotten my presence, until a pair of ducks drifts silently by, until anything upwind will have lost my scent. I stay until hunger reminds me that it's time to move on.

The way out takes me downwind, and to any animal in the area, once again I'm all smell and foreign presence. I'm also eyes and memory, which gives me my only edge over the stronger senses of animals. They depend primarily on scent for their cues, while humans, who rely primarily on vision, can see evidence that may be several years old, signs that have long since lost all defining odor. A coyote couldn't pick out the fact that a bear marked this tree, its distinctive claw prints identifying a claim to this place; nor could it read the naked branches above us, which a porcupine stripped clean sometime during the winter. The smells are gone, but the visual cues are as clear as words on a page.

It's the newer messages that trigger the stronger reactions, however, as with the coyote scat that's right in front of me, fresh and dark and different from scat in winter, when it's full of the hairy remains of old kills.

This is barely digested, wet and recent, probably left within the last hour or two.

I step quietly through the woods. On the hard dirt road, I can walk almost silently. But I can't mask the odors that give me away, and I can't read the more distant shadows.

I see no other sign of coyotes, and that's fine. I like the feel of my body on alert, ready for that leap across the trail, that gray or blond or burnished red streak, an animal in and out of safe edges. With such a desire urging me on, I know that soon I will track a coyote to its den. I'll smell the odor of scent posts and gut remains. I'll watch the pups pounce and worry, wrestle and hide, or gnaw on the bones the parents have tossed them, hoarding a knuckle-bone or favorite round rock.

And then, despite the swarm of blackflies and the hunger in my belly, I will back away, full of caution and joy, my want temporarily sated.

Epilogue

IN A COYOTE ENCLAVE in Stoneham, Massachusetts, five pups whirl about without ceasing. The one human they care about has arrived — Jonathan Way, who has played the role of parent since they were about twenty-four days old — and they can hardly contain their pleasure in his presence. They bang against his legs; they try to climb into his arms, his pockets, his shirt sleeves. They taste his face, his knees, his closely shaved head. They snarl with jealousy when another wriggles too close, as they each want to be in his lap, in his hands, in his full-focused attention.

In the picture I take of this greeting, his body, though long and sturdy, can hardly be seen amid theirs. Finally, the blast of welcome concluded, he tips back his head and howls. The others erupt into sound, five narrow muzzles aimed skyward in a yammering that multiplies their numbers, as though they are twenty animals, not five and one person.

The howl spirals out of the enclosure, past the maintenance workers, the joggers and strollers and kids shooting basketballs. It reaches drivers in their cars, parents putting children to sleep, and the many geese in the flock that drifts cautiously across the adjacent reservoir. The sound resonates with the wild coyotes as well, the ones seen within a mile of this zoo, and I imagine them pausing just long enough to consider the size of these youngsters and the yard that they must occupy before resuming their search for mice or good garbage.

The pups calm at last, busying themselves with the discovery and play that occupy most of their waking hours. Jon Way retrieves his clipboard and zeroes in on the pup he will observe for the next thirty minutes, recording its activity at fifteen-second intervals on a preset scale of relative engagement. His goal is simultaneously huge and minute. For now, he counts behaviors, which he will enter into a database; in the upcoming weeks and months he will analyze numbers and photographs and videotaped footage of the pups' activities beyond his line of sight. The overarching plan, however, is to do for coyotes what Jane Goodall has done for chimps and Dave Mech for wolves. He intends to provide the world with an array of intimate details about an intelligent, fascinating species, one to which he has been attuned since being tracked by a coyote near his home on Cape Cod.

He had been apple-baiting deer as part of an ecological study when he sensed he was being watched; soon he located the small coyote that continued to follow him from a safe distance as he worked. A year later he found and videotaped an active den on one of the Cape's barrier islands. A few years after that, finding little literature about the eastern coyote in suburban environments, he designed a graduate study on the ecology of Cape Cod coyotes. To find the evidence he wanted, he had to radio-collar the animals. "You can learn some general details without collaring," he points out. "If you want to know food habits, for example, you can simply study their scat. But to follow specific individuals, you have to radio-collar."

His timing for the project couldn't have been worse. Voters in Massachusetts, in passing the Wildlife Protection Act, had outlawed the kind of padded leghold traps that researchers prefer for capturing focus animals. (Contrary to public opinion, padded leghold traps seldom injure an animal; it's when the animal is left too long after being caught that it can fall prey to unleashed dogs and other predators, or it can wound or amputate its own legs in a desperate attempt to escape.) To secure research animals Way had to use large, seventy-pound box traps, which are obvious, easy to vandalize, and equally easy for adult coyotes to avoid entering. Other animals showed far less reluctance, however, and many of his predawn visits to check the traps yielded yet another sabotage in the form of raccoons, skunks, crows, opossums, red-tailed hawks, and vultures.

Soon, however, he perfected a technique for baiting the traps, using roadkill and grocery-supplied meats, and one by one he began capturing coyotes. The youngest animals had their radio transponders surgically implanted, as collars would quickly become too tight on their fast-growing bodies, while the larger coyotes were fitted with transponders around their necks. Then began the work of data recovery — a systematic recording of location done night and day, in summer and winter, most memorably in bitter cold hours when everyone else was warm and asleep. Traveling on foot or in his truck, Way tracked the traveling coyotes, assembling a record of each one's regular forays, which averaged about ten miles a night, through several different towns and many, many backyards.

In the last two years, he has expanded his study to that of coyotes in urban areas, this time within the I-95 beltway around Boston. Students from a local high-school science class have been enlisted to help him, yet though they have watched coyotes take bait near and just inside the traps, for the most part the animals have proven too wily to be caught. (The exceptions at the time of this writing include two animals collared in Revere, one of which was subsequently hit by a car, while the other died of a combination of starvation and hypothermia, brought on by a severe case of mange.)

THE PUP THAT WAY IS WATCHING still hasn't moved. The other four, though they could be anywhere within the 1,300-square-foot enclosure, choose to stay near him, wrestling against his legs, finding bones to chew within a few feet of where he stands, dashing off for a drink or a quick check of something — a noise, a smell, a shifting shadow — and then rushing back to be near his warmth and scent. The six of them have been together for almost four months, after Way pulled them out from under a shed in Falmouth, Massachusetts. They were about three and a half weeks old at the time, close to the stage when pups "start to know wildness." (At about four weeks old, they begin eating solid food and exploring the world outside their den, which means they would never have adjusted to a life spent in captivity, dependent on humans.) Way, delayed by bureaucratic compliance, arrived just in time.

The den was in a busy area, with two main roads nearby, and the pups' mother, seen sleeping in the backyard, was clearly habituated to people. (According to Way, it's the radio-collared coyotes that are the hardest to see, as they have learned to be wary of human intentions.) Way and a few volunteers excavated the den, the mother circling the yard all the while. Inside they found a total of nine pups, one of which was so tiny it seemed to be on the verge of starvation, perhaps from being trapped between floor joists where the parents couldn't reach it. Though the agreement with the Stone Zoo specified four pups, Way ultimately chose five — two males and three females, as one was the runt, and her chances of survival looked slim. The remaining four were returned to the den to be raised by their parents, with less competition for the food they brought in.

Taking up residence in a room at his grandparents', Way struggled to feed the pups through the first forty-eight hours. Several of them wouldn't nurse from a bottle, and they eschewed puppy formula; finally he started them on solid food at an age close to when they would have been offered it in the wild. They bonded, he says, when he brought them raw chicken, though their preference was for roadkill, which Way served in small pieces, much as a parent would. It was, he says, "a real pain to feed them."

For five weeks he kept up the routine; then the pups had to spend a mandatory thirty days in quarantine before being moved to the Sierra Madre exhibit at the Stone Zoo, a sizable acreage that includes separate enclosures for two mountain lions, two jaguars, and two endangered Mexican wolves.

I watch the pup that Way is watching (which still hasn't moved), while the unnatural sounds around us — particularly the sharp cries of a caged bird of prey — imply much about zoo life. This is now the permanent home of these pups. Soon the males will receive vasectomies, making life together easier for everyone concerned, and eventually the females might be spayed, though no final decision has yet been made about future reproduction. For now, the pups' whole joy seems connected with the presence of Jon Way and with the arrival of frozen mice and other treats from the zookeepers. The two pups who would disperse first if they were still in the wild — the two who don't need to be quite as close to him, who act more aloof as they circle the rocky grass yard — won't have the chance to explore a larger world. Part of the dynamic Way will observe is the behavior of coyotes when unnaturally confined, the hierarchy they establish and other ways they relate when they would like to be elsewhere. (I'm imagining the litter of siblings I grew up with, not sure how we would have managed had we been forced to stay under the same roof until old age.)

These pups, each with a name and a distinct personality, will have to do just fine. They'll surely adapt; they're coyotes, after all. Or so, at this point, we all assume.

When we first arrived at the enclosure, with its high fence and long plexiglass window for easy viewing, Way pointed out how similar in appearance the pups were to red wolves — tan with black-tipped hairs on their backs and tails, and distinctive red highlights on their muzzles, their ears, their thin legs. And then he sagged, the only time his energy waned in the several hours that we talked. His sigh was audible. "If these are hybrids, why are we calling them coyotes? Why not a species of wolf? Why not *Canis latrans lycaon* along with some new common name?"

One theory he has proposed is that there may be a coyote-wolf continuum, with true wolves at one end, true coyotes at the other, and various types showing up in between. But no one knows enough to support such a claim. (The confusion, after all, is at least a hundred years old, as evidenced in Teddy Roosevelt's *Outdoor Pastimes of an American Hunter:* "Big wolves and coyotes are found side by side throughout the Western United States, both varying so in size that if a sufficient number of specimens, from different localities, are examined it will be found that there is a complete intergradation in both stature and weight.")

Fortunately, surrounded by active coyote pups, Jon Way's confidence returned quickly. "Ecological studies will tell us more than genetics about the whole eastern coyote phenomenon," he insisted. His radio-collared animals on the Cape have already revealed much about species-specific rates of dispersal, territory size, and interactions with humans in suburban and urban settings. His captive pups should reveal similar details about such behaviors as socialization and degrees of bonding, along with the similarities and differences eastern coyotes share with gray wolves, red wolves, and western coyotes. (One myth they have already put to rest is about the supposed reluctance of eastern coyotes to socialize closely with people; clearly his pups think of Way as the best thing to come along since road-killed squirrel.)

THE THIRTY MINUTES ARE UP, Jon Way lowers his clipboard, and the watched pup is again on its feet, as quick to recover as an ill child after the school bus is out of sight.

Way enters the small enclosed area just off the pups' large yard, opens the gate, and motions me into the pen. Almost immediately, one of the pups pees on the pan of kibble. Another one, as soon as I sit down, leaps onto my back, nipping my ear, my arms, its teeth making contact but not breaking the skin, the same degree of gentleness the rest of them apply to the runt. They seem to sense our respective weaknesses — her brain didn't get enough food at critical moments, and I was born with thin skin, though with practice I could learn to hold my own against such pounding.

Soon the dusk starts to deepen, it's hard to see the enclosure's far edge, and the mosquitoes arrive just when Way predicted they would. We gather our gear and leave the pups to the unlikely sounds of this night — yaks and arctic foxes, eagles and jaguars, katydids and nighthawks and commercial jets high overhead.

Jon Way will be back tomorrow, as faithful to his charges as an instinct-driven parent, and I will shower and wash my clothes and still smell of coyotes two days later, a rankness that's slow to leave my skin.

Resources

Abbott, Kathleen. *Old Paths and Legends of the New England Border.* Knickerbocker Press, 1907.

Ackerman, Diane. *A Natural History of the Senses.* New York: Vintage, 1995.

Anderson, Peter. *In Search of the New England Coyote.* Chester, Connecticut: Globe Pequot Press, 1982.

Associated Press. "Wolf Reintroduction Debate Clouded by DNA Debate: Which Wolf?" *Forests.org*, Sept. 8, 2001. http://www.forests.org/archive/america/woredeba.htm.

Barry, Cynthia. "Wild Tales About America's Top Dog." *National Wildlife* (Feb.–Mar. 2001).

Bekoff, Marc. "Behavioral Development in Coyotes and Western Coyotes." In *Coyotes: Biology, Behavior, and Management*, edited by Marc Bekoff. New York: Academic Press, 1978.

———, ed. *Coyotes: Biology, Behavior, and Management.* New York: Academic Press, 1978.

Bekoff, Marc, and Michael C. Wells. "The Social Ecology of Coyotes." *Scientific American* (Apr. 1980). 130–148.

Boer, Arnold, ed. *Ecology and Management of the Eastern Coyote.* Fredericton, New Brunswick: Wildlife Research Unit, University of New Brunswick, 1992.

Bright, William. *A Coyote Reader.* Berkeley: University of California Press, 1993.

Bruchac, Joseph. *Native American Stories.* Golden, Colorado: Fulcrum Publishing, 1991.

Buell, Jeff. "Police Collar a Wily Intruder." *Daily Hampshire Gazette*, May 5, 1999.

Burt, William H., and Richard P. Grossenheider. *A Field Guide to Mammals.* The Peterson Field Guide Series. Boston: Houghton Mifflin, 1976.

Cadieux, Charles L. *Coyotes: Predators and Survivors.* Washington, DC: Stone Wall Press Inc., 1983.

Cardoza, James E., Gwilym S. Jones, Thomas W. French, and David B. Halliwell. *Massachusetts Exotic Vertebrates: Fauna of Massachusetts.* Series No. 6. Massachusetts Division of Fisheries and Wildlife, 1992.

Chambers, Robert E., Jr. "The Coyote in New York State." From the SUNY College of Environmental Science and Forestry Web site, http://www.esf.edu/pubprog/brochure/coyote/coyote.htm.

———. "A Howling Success: The Eastern Coyote." *New York State Conservationist* (August 2000).

———. "Reproduction of Coyotes in Their Northeastern Range." In *Ecology and Management of the Eastern Coyote*, edited by Arnold Boer. Fredericton, New Brunswick: Wildlife Research Unit, University of New Brunswick, 1992.

Cole, John N. "The Return of the Coyote." *Harper's Magazine* (May 1973).

Conuel, Thomas. *Quabbin: The Accidental Wilderness.* Revised ed. Amherst: University of Massachusetts Press, 1990.

Coppinger, Raymond, and Lorna Coppinger. *Dogs: A Startling New Understanding of Canine Origin, Behavior and Evolution.* New York: Scribner's, 2001.

Coppinger, Raymond P., Ph.D., Michael Sands, and Emily Groves. "Meet New England's New Wolf." *Massachusetts Wildlife* (summer, 1973).

Cronon, William. *Changes in the Land: Indians, Colonists, and the Ecology of New England.* New York: Hill and Wang, 1983.

Derr, Mark. "Growing Bigger Coyotes." *Audubon* (Nov.–Dec. 1994).

Dizard, Jan E. *Going Wild: Hunting, Animal Rights, and the Con-*

tested Meaning of Nature. Amherst: University of Massachusetts Press, 1994.

Echeverria, Jaime. "Existence Values for Bald Eagle, Coyote and Wild Turkey in New England." Unpublished thesis, University of Massachusetts at Amherst, 1990.

Evans, Arthur B., and Charles L. Bellamy. *An Inordinate Fondness for Beetles*. New York: Henry Holt, 1996.

Fabre, Jean Henri. *The Insect World of J. Henri Fabre*, edited by Edwin Way Teale. New York: Dodd, Mead, 1961.

Finkel, Mike. "The Ultimate Survivor." *Audubon* (May 1999). 101:3.

Forbush, Edward Howe. *Birds of Massachusetts and Other New England States*. Vols. I–III. Massachusetts Department of Agriculture, 1925.

Foster, David F. *Thoreau's Country: Journey Through a Transformed Landscape*. Cambridge, MA: Harvard University Press, 1999.

Gaskell, Elizabeth. *The Life of Charlotte Brontë*. New York: Penguin, 1975.

Grooms, Steve. *The Return of the Wolf*. Minocqua, WI: NorthWord Press, 1993.

Hampton, Bruce. *The Great American Wolf*. New York: Henry Holt & Co., 1997.

Harrison, Daniel J. "Social Ecology of Coyotes in Northeastern North America: Relationships to Dispersal, Food Resources, and Human Exploitation." In *Ecology and Management of the Eastern Coyote*, edited by Arnold Boer. Fredericton, New Brunswick: Wildlife Research Unit, University of New Brunswick, 1992.

Hilton, Henry. "Systematics and Ecology of the Eastern Coyote." In *Coyotes: Biology, Behavior, and Management*, edited by Marc Bekoff. New York: Academic Press, 1978.

———. "Coyotes in Maine: A Case Study." In *Ecology and Management of the Eastern Coyote*, edited by Arnold Boer. Fredericton, New Brunswick: Wildlife Research Unit, University of New Brunswick, 1992.

Hoagland, Edward. "Lament the Red Wolf." In *Heart's Desire*. New York: Simon & Schuster, 1988.

Hogan, Linda. "Deify the Wolf." In *Dwellings: A Spiritual History of the Natural World*. New York: Norton, 1995.

Hossler, Sam. "Deer Biology: Where Do All the Fawns Go?" *Deer & Deer Hunting* (June 2002).

Hubbell, Sue. *Broadsides from the Other Orders: A Book of Bugs*. Boston: Houghton Mifflin, 1993.

Hughes, John. "The Curse Environment." *The Orange County Register* (Santa Ana, CA), Sept. 21, 1997, p. E01 (Stuart Ellins's findings on coyotes communicating news of tainted sheep meat).

Leahy, Christopher W., John Hanson Mitchell, and Thomas Conuel. *The Nature of Massachusetts*. Reading, MA: Addison-Wesley Publishing Co. for Massachusetts Audubon Society, 1996.

Lehner, Philip N. "Coyote Communication." In *Coyotes: Biology, Behavior, and Management*, edited by Marc Bekoff. New York: Academic Press, 1978.

Leland, Charles G. *The Algonquin Legends of New England; or, Myths and Folk Lore of the Micmac, Passamaquoddy, and Penobscot Tribes*. Boston: Houghton, Mifflin and Co., 1884.

Lopez, Barry Holstun. *Of Wolves and Men*. New York: Charles Scribner's Sons, 1978.

Lorenz, Jay Ronald. "Physical Characteristics, Movement, and Population Estimate of the Eastern Coyote in New England." Master's thesis, University of Massachusetts, 1978.

Massachusetts Department of Fisheries & Wildlife. *Annual Reports*, 1955–1996.

Miniter, Frank. "Predator Wars: Part I. The Duel." *Outdoor Life* (Dec.–Jan. 1999); and "Predator Wars: Part II. Preying on People." *Outdoor Life* (Feb. 1999).

Mirick, Peter G. "Coyotes and Other Questions." *Massachusetts Wildlife*. 98:4, 10–23.

Moore, Gary C., and Gerry R. Parker. "Colonization by the Eastern Coyote *(Canis Latrans)*." In *Ecology and Management of the Eastern Coyote*, edited by Arnold Boer. Fredericton, New Brunswick: Wildlife Research Unit, University of New Brunswick, 1992.

Mourning Dove. *Coyote Stories*. Lincoln: University of Nebraska Press, [1933] 1990.

Murie, Olaus J. *A Field Guide to Animal Tracks*. The Peterson Field Guide Series. Boston: Houghton Mifflin, 1954, rev. 1974.

Myers, K. C. "Coyote Shot After Attacking Toddler." *Cape Cod Times* (Hyannis, MA), July 30, 1998.

Nelson, Richard. *Heart and Blood: Living with Deer in America*. New York: Knopf, 1997.

———. *The Island Within*. New York: North Point Press, 1989.

Nolan, Lori A. "Coyotes Mark Their Territory: Cape Cod." *Cape Cod Times*, June 6, 2000.

Nowak, Ron. "Hybridization: The Double-Edged Threat." *Canid News*, vol. 3, 1995, http://www.canids.org/PUBLICAT/CNDNEWS3/hybridiz.htm.

Orwell, George. "Shooting An Elephant." In *Multitude: Cross-Cultural Readings for Writers*, edited by Chitra Divakaruni. New York: McGraw Hill, 1993.

Parker, G. R. *Eastern Coyote: The Story of Its Success*. Halifax, Nova Scotia: Nimbus Publishing, 1995.

Patterson, Brent. "Deer-Coyote Study." In *Conservation*, vols. 1 and 2. Nova Scotia Department of Natural Resources, winter, 1998.

Pekins, Peter J. "Winter Diet and Bioenergetics of Eastern Coyotes: A Review." In *Ecology and Management of the Eastern Coyote*, edited by Arnold Boer. Fredericton, New Brunswick: Wildlife Research Unit, University of New Brunswick, 1992.

Person, D. K., and D. H. Hirth. "Home Range and Habitat Use of Coyotes in a Farm Region of Vermont." *Journal of Wildlife Management* (1991). 55:433–441.

Pistorius, Alan. "Coyotes on the Move." *Northern Woodlands* (autumn, 2002).

Pringle, Larry. "Stranger from the West." *Massachusetts Wildlife* (May–June 1959).

Rezendes, Paul. *Tracking and the Art of Seeing: How to Read Animal Tracks and Sign.* 2nd ed. New York: HarperCollins, 1999.

Roosevelt, Theodore. *Outdoor Pastimes of an American Hunter.* New York: Scribner's, 1920.

Ryden, Hope. *God's Dog: The North American Coyote.* New York: Lyons Press, 1997 (originally published in 1979).

Sabean, Barry. "Coyotes & Deer." In *Conservation.* Nova Scotia Department of Natural Resources, spring, 1991, http://www.gov.ns.ca/natr/wildlife/conserva/15-01-9.htm.

Stevens, Thomas H., Thomas A. More, and Ronald J. Glass. "Public Attitudes About Coyotes in New England." *Society and Natural Resources* (1994). 7:57–66.

Stewart, Frank. *A Natural History of Nature Writing.* Washington, DC: Island Press, 1995 ("99% of the life forms that have ever lived are now extinct").

Suplee, Curt. "Study Dates House Dogs to 100,000 Years Ago. DNA Suggests Wild Wolves Bred Primordial Pooch Far Earlier Than Believed." *The Washington Post,* June 13, 1997, p. A3.

Theberge, John B. and Mary T. *Wolf Country: Eleven Years Tracking the Algonquin Wolves.* Toronto: McClelland & Stewart, 1998.

Thoreau, Henry David. *Journal* VIII (March 23, 1856: "When I consider the nobler animals have been exterminated here . . .").

Tullar, Ben. "Eastern Coyote — Always a New York Native." *Conservationist* (Jan.–Feb. 1992). 34–39.

Twain, Mark. *Roughing It.* New York: New American Library, 1980.

U.S. Fish and Wildlife Service, Division of Endangered Species. "Red Wolf." In *Endangered and Threatened Species of the Southeastern United States (The Red Book)*, FWS Region 4 (as of Aug. 1993), http://endangered.fws.gov/i/a/saa04.html.

Wade, Nicholas. "From Wolf to Dog, Yes, But When?" *New York Times*, November 22, 2002.

Way, Jonathan. "Coyote Research on Cape Cod," *Massachusetts Wildlife.* 98:4, 25–27.

———. "The Eastern Coyote: Documenting the Habits of One of Cape Cod's Newest Residents," *Conservation Perspectives* (spring, 2001), http://www.massscb.org/epublications/spring2001/coyotes.html.

Wayne, Bob. "Red Wolves: To Conserve or Not to Conserve." *Canid News* (1995). Vol. 3, http://www.canids.org/PUBLICAT/CNDNEWS3/2conserv.htm.

Wayne, Robert K., and Niles Lehman. "Mitochondrial DNA Analysis of the Eastern Coyote: Origins and Hybridization." In *Ecology and Management of the Eastern Coyote*, edited by Arnold Boer. Fredericton, New Brunswick: Wildlife Research Unit, University of New Brunswick, 1992.

Weidensaul, Scott. *Living on the Wind: Across the Hemisphere with Migratory Birds.* New York: North Point Press, 1999.

Weiner, Jonathan. *The Beak of the Finch.* New York: Vintage Books, 1995.

Williams, Ted. "Maine's War on Coyotes." *Audubon Magazine* (Sept. 2002).

Wood, William. *New England's Prospect.* Edited by Alden T. Vaughan. Amherst: University of Massachusetts Press, 1977.

Acknowledgments

Many people helped move this project from a vague idea into something that could be held and shared, and I thank each for playing such a significant role in this process. The encouragement I received from those who read early drafts — Susie Patlove, Mary Clare Powell, Trish Crapo, and my sister, Liza O'Neil — provided a necessary momentum, while both Michelle Hoover and Michelle Valois offered valuable feedback on manuscript quandaries. I was fortunate to have met two different scientists when I did — Elijah Goodwin, whose expertise as an evolutionary biologist aided my understanding of mutualism, hybridization, and some of the limits of DNA testing, and Pat Serrentino, ornithologist and well-versed naturalist, whose generous reading of the manuscript has assured a measure of accuracy. Any errors that remain are now mine alone.

I am very much indebted to all those who shared sightings and ideas about this new animal in our midst — Joan Deely, who described her work helping skin carcasses, scrape hides, and weigh and measure skulls as part of Ray Coppinger's work on the "New Wolf" in the 1970s; Grace Edwards, Jack Haley, Jack Masson, Diane Olanyk, and Rebekkah Tippens for details of their various coyote encounters; and Kathy O'Rourke for her essay "Listening the Navajo Way" and for elaborating on the way a coyote might convey a message.

I am sincerely grateful for the work of Paul Rezendes, who has introduced thousands of people to the world of tracking and reading animal sign. John Foster, founder of the New England

Naturalist Training Center, delighted me with specifics of some of his coyote sightings, including those of a black coyote and of a coyote sleeping in the trail. MassWildlife's Ellie Horwitz and Tom French answered many of my questions and provided additional anecdotes, as did Dave Rich of the state's environmental police force. John Hall and Kimberly Royar, from Vermont's Department of Fish and Wildlife, volunteered provocative insights about the changing nature of this animal, including whether, two decades from now, we will even call this an "eastern coyote."

Jonathan Way provided a wealth of information specific to *Canis latrans* as I observed him interact with the litter of young coyotes he is raising as part of a long-term behavioral study. I am grateful to him for his dedication to the species.

For making their libraries such essential local resources, I thank Louis Battalen of the Arms Library in Shelburne Falls (along with Karen Racz for help during her tenure there) and Carol Letson, Hope Schneider, and Carolyn Bellany of Greenfield Community College. I am also much appreciative of the regulars at the Arms Library monthly reading series for their immediate and positive feedback, and of Don Williams, editor of *New Millennium Writings*, and Melanie Bishop, editor of *Alligator Juniper*, for choosing excerpts as winners of their creative nonfiction awards ("The Return" and "Body of the Story," respectively).

I also thank three men whose quirky pleasures were infectious and whom I wished had lived long enough to see this work published — Jerry Stern, director of the creative writing program at Florida State University, for the hours at St. Mark's Wildlife Refuge and the push to pursue the writing of nonfiction; Chuck Zerby, poet and enthusiast extraordinaire, for reading early chapters and dubbing me a "singer of scat"; and Karl Davies, steward of northern forests, for weighing in on several of these ideas as we traversed the hills around Mount Toby.

To the trail companions with whom I went forth at differ-

ent times — Geoff Brock, Peggy Hart, Chloe Reid, and Christa
Longo — thanks for the camaraderie; the discoveries were better
because you were there. To the creative writing students who
inspired me with their talents and insights — at Florida State
University, Greenfield Community College, and in the "Sense of
Place" class at Stoneleigh-Burnham School — thanks for braving
the prompts and producing such strong work. And thanks to Diane and John at Diversified Computers in Keene for their efficient
repairs, both post-mischief and post-lightning strike.

For their unwavering support of this project, I thank both my
agent, Kit Ward, and my editor, Deanne Urmy. Their patience
and vision have proven invaluable, and the book is far better for
their care of it.

Finally, and with great appreciation, I thank my family for
their myriad forms of support — my parents, who provided the
early field guides and unflagging interest in new discoveries; my
grandmother, who started me birding when I was six or seven; and
my siblings, Bob, Arthur, Liza, Douglas, and Cindy, all of whom
helped shape this work in ways large and small. (And to think this
might have started with the journal we kept at the cabin, "Caught
two trout. Watched three beaver. Saw bear tracks but never saw
the bear.")

And to Holly Iglesias, who has brought such joy into my life:
thanks for believing in this idea from the night of that very first
howl, and for that moment long before when you risked the big
leap.